AP® WORLD HISTORY: MODERN CRASH COURSE®

By Jay P. Harmon, M.Ed.

T0204784

 Research & Education Association
www.rea.com

Research & Education Association
258 Prospect Plains Road
Cranbury, New Jersey 08512
Email: info@rea.com

AP® WORLD HISTORY: MODERN
CRASH COURSE,® 3rd Edition

Printed in the United States of America

Library of Congress Control Number 2019949057

ISBN-13: 978-0-7386-1261-4
ISBN-10: 0-7386-1261-8

Cover image: © iStockphoto.com/JacobAmmentorpLund

AP® WORLD HISTORY: MODERN CRASH COURSE
TABLE OF CONTENTS

PART I   INTRODUCTION

PART II   **Chronological Review**

PART III

Review Charts

PART IV

Test-Taking Strategies and Practice Questions

ABOUT OUR BOOK

REA's *AP® World History: Modern Crash Course* is designed for the last-minute studier or any student who wants a quick refresher on the AP® course. The *Crash Course* is based on the 2019–2020 AP® World History: Modern course and exam and focuses only on the topics tested, so you can make the most of your study time.

Written by a nationally recognized AP® World History test expert, our *Crash Course* gives you a concise review of the major concepts and important topics tested on the AP® exam.

- **Part I** offers you our **Keys for Success**, so you can tackle the exam with confidence. It also gives you a list of important terms that you absolutely must know.

- **Part II** is a **Chronological Review** that covers all of the periods found in the AP® World History: Modern course framework.

- **Part III** reveals the **Key Concepts and Themes** to remind you of the important overall developments throughout World History.

- **Part IV** explains the format of the exam and offers specific **Test-Taking Strategies** to conquer the multiple-choice and short-answer questions, the Document-Based Question, and the long essay. You'll also find AP®-style practice questions to prepare you for what you'll see on test day.

ABOUT OUR ONLINE PRACTICE EXAM

How ready are you for the AP® World History: Modern exam? Find out by taking REA's online practice exam. To access your practice exam, visit the online REA Study Center (*www.rea.com/studycenter*). This test features automatic scoring, detailed explanations of all answers, and diagnostic score reporting that will help you identify your strengths and weaknesses so you'll be ready on exam day.

Whether you use this book throughout the school year or as a refresher in the final weeks before the exam, REA's *Crash Course* will show you how to study efficiently and strategically, so you can boost your score.

Good luck on your AP® World History: Modern exam!

ABOUT OUR AUTHOR

Jay P. Harmon teaches AP® World History: Modern at Houston Christian High School in Houston, Texas. A veteran teacher, he has been one of the most sought-after AP® history presenters in the United States and abroad.

Mr. Harmon served as a leader of the AP® World History evaluation program since its inception in 2002. A former member of the AP® World History Test Development Committee, he was an AP® consultant to the College Board for 17 years.

His AP® World History website (*http://ap.harmonhistory.com*) is considered an essential resource for APWH teachers the world over.

In 2016, Mr. Harmon traveled to South Korea as the guest of the Academy of Korean Studies, joining with AP® World History gurus Patrick Whelan and Barbara Ozuna to offer insights into the AP® program. In 2019, he was invited back to South Korea to mark the 15th anniversary of the Understanding Korea Project.

Mr. Harmon earned his B.S. and M.Ed. degrees from Louisiana State University. He began his teaching career in 1982 and has taught in public and private schools in Louisiana and Texas.

I would like to extend my special thanks to my wife, Monica, my sons, Joey and Christopher, the faculty and staff at Houston Christian High School, my A4 and B2 classes, and Ga Young Seo and Katherine Kovach for their support on this exciting project.—JPH

ACKNOWLEDGMENTS

We would like to thank Larry B. Kling, Editorial Director, for his overall guidance; Pam Weston, Publisher, for setting the quality standards for production integrity and managing the publication to completion; John Paul Cording, Technology Director; and Wayne Barr, Test Prep Project Manager, for shepherding this book through development.

We would also like to extend our appreciation to Gabe Fain and Joanna Cone for technically reviewing the manuscript; Diane Goldschmidt for copyediting; Kathy Caratozzolo of Caragraphics for typesetting; and Jennifer Calhoun for file prep.

PART I

INTRODUCTION

Eight Keys to Success
on the AP® World History:
Modern Exam

"So . . . what do I need to know?" you're asking yourself. Oh, not much . . . only about 800 years of global history. Wait, don't throw away this book and run screaming from the room. First, take a deep breath and examine the facts: More than 300,000 high school students just like you will take the AP® World History: Modern exam this school year and about half of them will earn college credit. *Why not you?* You're clearly a clever and motivated person—after all, you're reading this *Crash Course* study guide.

Good news: You don't have to know *everything* from around 1200 CE to the early 2000s to do well on the AP® World History: Modern exam. By studying efficiently and strategically, you can get college credit and add that special AP®-credit sparkle to your transcript. This book will help you understand and use the following keys to success:

1. **Know the Content of the Exam**

    The AP® World History: Modern exam content is divided into the following chronological categories. "Exam weight" refers to the percentage of the exam that will come from each historical period.

Units	Historical Periods	Exam Weight
Unit 1: The Global Tapestry	c. 1200 to c. 1450	8%–10%
Unit 2: Networks of Exchange	c. 1200 to c. 1450	8%–10%
Unit 3: Land-Based Empires	c. 1450 to c. 1750	12%–15%
Unit 4: Transoceanic Interconnections	c. 1450 to c. 1750	12%–15%

(continued)

Units	Historical Periods	Exam Weight
Unit 5: Revolutions	c. 1750 to c. 1900	12%–15%
Unit 6: Consequences of Industrialization	c. 1750 to c. 1900	12%–15%
Unit 7: Global Conflict	c. 1900 to the present	8%–10%
Unit 8: Cold War and Decolonization	c. 1900 to the present	8%–10%
Unit 9: Globalization	c. 1900 to the present	8%–10%

A close look at the chart, for example, reveals that the era c. 1200–c. 1450 is only 16% to 20% of the exam. This helps you focus your plan of study. In addition, though the AP® World History: Modern exam states that it covers human history "to the present," the reality is that you shouldn't expect any exam questions past 2001. Look at the chart again. The 20th century is divided into three units that cover up to 30% of the exam. So you can't take the 20th century lightly.

The latest updates to AP® World History: Modern exam content and structure can be found at *http://apcentral.collegeboard.org*.

2. **Know Your Competition**

Don't be intimidated by your competition—you have an advantage over most students by paying attention to the guidance in this book. About 80% of students who take the AP® World History: Modern exam are sophomores, and most of them are taking their first AP® exam. The next biggest group is composed of freshmen, then juniors and seniors. Typically about *half* of all AP® World History test-takers pass the exam and get college credit by scoring a 3, 4, or 5 on a scale of 1 to 5.

Caution: Even though a passing score may seem easily attainable, don't get overconfident and think you've got it made. Taking an AP® exam and receiving college credit takes *a lot* of focused work. You need serious, organized preparation to be successful.

3. Know the Format of the Exam and How it is Scored

The AP® World History: Modern exam has two main parts: **Section I**, which consists of multiple-choice questions and short-answer questions, and **Section II**, which has two essay questions. The multiple-choice portion is scored by machine, contains 55 questions, and must be completed in 55 minutes. It is worth 40% of the total exam score. Just like any multiple-choice test, you will answer some questions very quickly and others will take more time. When the multiple-choice part of the exam is over, you will then have 40 minutes to answer three out of four short-answer questions, worth 20% of the total exam score. Then you will have a short break and return for the essay part of the exam. Bring a snack and a bottle of water for the break.

In Section II of the exam, you will write two essays: a document-based question (DBQ) and a long essay. You will have 100 minutes to complete both essays. The DBQ is worth 25% of your overall score and the long essay is worth 15%. Each essay is read and scored by a trained AP® World History teacher or a World History college professor. Your essay scores are then added to your Section I scores to arrive at your final AP® score.

You'll find more tips about tackling the multiple-choice and short-answer questions, as well as the essays, in the discussions about test-taking strategies found in Part IV of this book.

4. Know What Your Final Score Means

The College Board uses a formula to rank your combined multiple-choice, short-answer, and free-response score into five categories:

5 = Extremely Well Qualified

4 = Well Qualified

3 = Qualified

2 = Possibly Qualified

1 = No Recommendation

A 3 on all AP® exams is considered a passing grade. About 10% of AP® World History: Modern test-takers earn the top score of 5, but keep reading—the scoring range is more generous than you think. If you get about half of the exam's multiple-choice questions right, earn about 4 out of 9 possible points on the short-answer questions, and earn about half of the points on the two essays, you should reach a 3. That doesn't mean the exam is easy—the opposite is true.

In AP® World History, about half of all test-takers have typically made a "3" or better. Many colleges award course credit for a score of 3; other colleges take nothing below a 4, while still others give college credit only for 5's. Be aware that colleges and universities can change their AP® acceptance policies whenever they want. Stay up-to-date by checking the AP® policies on their websites.

5. Know How AP® World History: Modern Is Different from Traditional World History

You might think that history is history, but AP® World History: Modern is different from traditional approaches: Learning lists of "Kings and Wars" or "The West and the Rest" doesn't cut it. The AP® World History: Modern test developers want you to see the big picture. They want you to make connections across the globe and across time and to analyze common human experiences like migration, trade, religion, politics, and society. Think of it this way: Studying AP® World History: Modern is like learning American History. You don't examine the histories of 50 individual states— instead you learn about the important themes, people, and events of the 50 states together. The same idea applies to AP® World History: Modern—think globally, not nationally, and you'll do well.

Bear in mind: If your World History textbook doesn't say "Advanced Placement®" or "AP®" on the cover, look at the introduction to see whether the authors discuss concepts like global history and making connections between civilizations across time and place. If not, you may need to find a different textbook that explains history in these ways.

6. Know What You Don't Need to Know

Nobody expects you to know everything about World History since the year 1200 in order to do well on the AP® exam. AP® World History: Modern is more about the big picture than the little details. That means you don't need to memorize all the emperors of China, the battles of the Crimean War, or the name of Napoleon's horse (Marengo, by the way).

7. **Know How to Use This *Crash Course* to Build a Plan for Success**

   This *Crash Course* is based on a careful study of the trends in both course study and exam content.

   In Part I, you'll be introduced to the AP® World History: Modern course and exam. In Chapter 2, you'll find a list of key terms, concepts, and themes you should know for success. Chapter 3 gives you a brief overview of the course.

   In Part II (Chapters 4–12) you will find chronological reviews of important political, economic, cultural, environmental, and social connections in world history. These reviews are based on the current AP® World History: Modern Course and Exam Description—the College Board's guide for teachers and exam creators. Coverage overlaps from chapter to chapter for the sake of reinforcement.

   Part III (Chapters 13–16), includes review charts and tables designed to help you make important connections across time and place.

   Finally, Part IV (Chapters 17–22) prepares you to take the exam by giving you insider test-taking strategies for the multiple-choice questions, the short-answer questions, the document-based question (DBQ), and the long-essay question.

8. **Know How to Supplement This *Crash Course***

   This *Crash Course* contains what you need to do well on the AP® World History: Modern exam. You should, however, supplement it with other materials designed specifically for studying AP® World History: Modern. Visit the College Board's AP® Central website for more information and practice. And don't forget the online practice exam that comes with this book, complete with detailed answers.

Concepts, Themes, and Key Terms

OVERARCHING CONCEPTS

1. HISTORICAL THINKING SKILLS

The AP® World History: Modern course and exam require you to understand and use six key historical thinking skills. This means that you're being asked to think like a historian. As a result, you're expected to approach the exam equipped to do the following. We'll have more to say on these skills later.

SKILL 1. Identify and explain historical developments and processes.

➤ Why do events and processes in history happen?

SKILL 2. Analyze sourcing and situation of primary and secondary sources.

➤ Understand the point of view (POV) of documents.

SKILL 3. Analyze arguments in primary and secondary sources.

➤ Explain why historians have different opinions about historical events.

SKILL 4. Analyze the context of historical events, developments, or processes.

➤ Understand that history does not happen in a vacuum.

SKILL 5. Using historical reasoning processes (see below), analyze patterns and connections between and among historical developments and processes.

➤ Make sense of history with connections that go beyond facts.

SKILL 6. Develop an argument.

➤ Take a stand on historical issues using supporting evidence.

2. HISTORICAL REASONING PROCESSES

In reasoning like a historian, you hone an approach that shapes how you think. The following are the reasoning processes historians—and AP® World History: Modern exam candidates—use.

A. **Comparison:** Analyze similarities and differences between historical developments and processes.

B. **Causation:** Describe causes and effects of historical developments and processes and their significance; explain the context of historical developments.

C. **Continuity and Change:** Explain the significance of historical developments in patterns of change and continuity over time.

WORLD HISTORY: MODERN THEMES

Six themes run through the course. These themes are the broad ideas that connect events to the bigger picture of world history. Apply them to gain a deeper understanding, going beyond knowledge of historical facts.

Theme 1: Humans and the Environment

➤ The ways the physical environment (rivers, mountains, weather, ecology, etc.) and humans interact. For example, many cities developed near rivers so the water could be used for crops and transportation.

➤ Human population and its effects on the environment.

Theme 2: Cultural Developments and Interactions

➤ Beliefs, religions, ideas, art and what they reveal about societies.

➤ The political, social and cultural effects of interactions of these ideas between societies.

Theme 3: Governance

➤ Different forms of government: their rise, maintenance, and decline.

➤ How governments maintain order and exercise power.

Theme 4: Economic Systems

➤ The societies produce, exchange, and consume goods and services, and the effects of same.

Theme 5: Social Interactions and Organization

➤ How societies establish norms of behavior for groups and individuals, and how these norms change or stay constant over time.

➤ The political, economic, and cultural interactions and influences of those norms.

Theme 6: Technology and Innovation

➤ How human adaptation and innovation results in increased efficiency, comfort, and security and how technological advances have shaped human development with both intended and unintended consequences.

KEY TERMS

UNITS 1 AND 2 | THE GLOBAL TAPESTRY AND NETWORKS OF EXCHANGE: c. 1200 to c. 1450

1. **CHINESE DYNASTIES**—From well before the 13th century to the early 20th century, China was governed by a series of families that ruled for long periods. The Song Dynasty was important, declining in the late 13th century (see Chapter 4).

2. **HINDUISM**—The earliest known organized religion dating back some 4,000 years, with written codes of the faith and a class of religious leaders (priests). Hinduism was centered in South Asia. Hindu teachings supported the caste system that greatly influenced the political and social structure of South Asia.

3. **BUDDHISM**—A "reform" of Hinduism begun by Prince Siddhartha Gautama c. 500 BCE, who became the Buddha ("Enlightened One"). Unlike Hinduism, Buddhism supported spiritual equality and missionary activity. Its two most popular forms, Mahayana and Theravada Buddhism, spread far from its origins in South Asia into Southeast and East Asia along trade routes, bringing significant cultural effects that last to this day. Hindu- and Buddhist-dominated states, such as the Srivijaya Empire, arose in Southeast Asia.

4. **CONFUCIANISM**—In the 6th century BCE, the Chinese philosopher Confucius established clearly defined codes of behavior and gender and family duties. His teachings were a philosophy, not a religion dedicated to a deity. Over time, however, Neo-Confucianism emerged in East Asia. It included aspects of Buddhism and the ancient Chinese belief system Daoism, promising eternal reward for faithfulness to Confucian teachings. Neo-Confucianism became prominent during the Song Dynasty in China and spread to Japan and Korea.

5. **ANIMISM/POLYTHEISM/SHAMANISM**—The earliest known form of religion, animism, sees gods in nature (worshipping the sun, for example). It was popular among hunting-foraging bands. Animism is related to shamanism, in which a human guide engages in the spirit world to ask for rain, for example. Forms of animism remain today. Polytheism ("many gods") differs from animism in that gods in polytheism have specific names and duties.

6. **MONOTHEISM**—Monotheism is the belief in one god. The Hebrews of Southwest Asia practiced one of the earliest known monotheistic religions, Judaism.

7. **CHRISTIANITY**—As Buddhism was to Hinduism, Christianity was a reform of an existing religion, Judaism. Jesus taught eternal salvation through the belief that he was the Jewish Messiah, sent by God to save humanity from eternal punishment. Over time, missionaries spread Jesus's gospel ("good news") throughout the Roman Empire and beyond. Christianity, Buddhism, and Islam spread globally and are the religions with the most followers today.

8. **ISLAM**—This religion was first preached in Arabia in the seventh century CE by the prophet Muhammad. Islam ("submission") united many polytheistic Arab tribes into a common faith. By the mid-700s, it had spread rapidly through conquest and missionary activity via trade routes out of Southwest Asia across North Africa to Spain and eastward into northern India and Central Asia. Over time Muslim merchants carried Islam into Southeast and East Asia.

9. **DAR AL-ISLAM**—Across Afro-Eurasia, Dar al-Islam means "everywhere Islam is." In the era c. 1200–c. 1450, this term described the territory extending from Spain and Northwest Africa

all the way to South and Southeast Asia. Dar al-Islam was not a unified political empire, but a large region where Islamic faith and culture was dominant.

10. **CALIPHATE**—Unlike Christianity, Islam had no clear rules of succession after Muhammad. Culturally, Islam united many peoples, but politically, it fragmented into regional states called caliphates, each led by a caliph. The Abbasid caliphate ruled from Baghdad until it was sacked by the Mongols in 1258.

11. **TURKIC PEOPLES**—Central Asian nomadic peoples who had a common language family called Turkish. Their migrations into Southwest Asia beginning in the 10th century ushered in a period of political domination by Turkish groups such as the Seljuk and later the Ottomans that lasted until the 20th century. These Turkish groups converted to Islam and established regional states called sultanates, named after the leader of the Turkish group, a Sultan.

12. **DIFFUSION OF RELIGIONS**—Before 1450, three religions spread far outside their places of origin: Christianity, Buddhism, and Islam. Buddhism and Christianity were spread by missionary monks. Conversions to Christianity and Islam were also done by "sword mission," meaning by force. Like Buddhism and Christianity, Islam was also spread peacefully by merchants along trade routes.

13. **SYNCRETISM IN RELIGIONS**—A global religion must be flexible enough to adapt to local customs as it spreads. Many examples of the global diffusion of religion exist: when Buddhism spread into East Asia, the Buddha became a god-like provider of eternal salvation; as Islam spread into parts of South Asia, it adopted some Hindu features and turned toward mysticism with Sufism; some forms of Christianity in the New World adopted traditional gods and made them part of the pantheon of saints.

14. **THE SILK ROADS**—A must-know trade route, the Silk Roads connected East Asia to northern India and central Asia and, indirectly, to the Mediterranean region, West Africa, and northern Europe. Silk, tea, spices, belief systems, and technology were carried westward along caravan routes. Chinese goods and technology made their way into southwest Asia, Africa, and Europe.

15. **INDIAN OCEAN TRADE NETWORK**—Connected to the Silk Roads, the Indian Ocean trade network was just as important, but with routes over water. Ships tended to carry heavier bulk items than were transported on the Silk Roads—for example, lumber and pottery. African, Arab, Jewish, and Chinese (both Muslim and Christian) merchants transmitted religion (especially Buddhism and Islam) and exchanged silver, cotton, spices, and many other items across the Indian Ocean. Seasonal monsoon winds aided sailing ships in the Indian Ocean.

16. **TRANS-SAHARAN TRADE**—The trade of goods, people, and faith across North Africa's Sahara desert peaked in the 8th to the 16th centuries. Gold, salt, animal hides, and slaves were among the main items transported by camel from Africa to points east and north. Muslim merchants imported camels into the region; they also brought their faith in Islam, which spread rapidly into North and West Africa. Three important West African trade centers along these trade routes were Djenné, Goa, and Timbuktu.

17. **WEST AFRICAN KINGDOMS**—Muslim West African kingdoms like Mali facilitated exchanges between Africa, Europe, and Asia. Mali was a center for gold and salt trade. Its most famous leader was Mansa Musa, who traveled to Mecca in a fabulously rich caravan in the 14th century.

18. **BYZANTINE EMPIRE**—Based in Constantinople, this empire, which traced its beginnings back to the classical Roman Empire, had major economic, social, and political influence over southern and eastern Europe, the Eastern Mediterranean, and Southwest Asia until it was conquered and ended by Muslim forces in 1453. Culturally, it was the center of Orthodox Christianity, one of the major branches of the faith.

19. **ETHIOPIA**—One of the greatest African empires, founded in East Africa, and largely Christian. It had many connections to Christian European and Muslim interests beginning before c. 1200 and continuing today.

20. **MONGOLS**—"Agents of change" or "an unstoppable tide of horror"—both definitions accurately describe the Mongols. In the

13th century, Mongol forces invaded south China and rode west all the way into Russia and Southwest Asia. After usually brutal conquests, they established a Pax Mongolica: peace and trade throughout their territories, which was the largest land empire ever established. The united Mongol empire was short-lived, however, and even the khanates that splintered from it faded in political power by the 15th century.

21. **BUBONIC PLAGUE**—The bubonic plague, also known as the Black Death, is arguably history's most infamous disease. Possibly originating along the trade routes near the Black Sea, it spread east and west during the age of the Mongol conquests, killing millions. Striking in the mid-14th century, the bubonic plague is widely believed to have wiped out as much as one-third of the population of Europe, China, and Central Asia.

22. **MAYAN STATES**—The Mayan States were centered in Mesoamerica (Southern Mexico and part of Central America). Mayans had cities with tall stone buildings, a written language and a complex society. Its government fell in the 10th century, but its culture—especially its religion and spoken language—continued for centuries more.

23. **COERCED LABOR**—Includes slavery, serfdom, the corvée (government-required labor on public works projects), and indentured servitude. Forms of coerced labor existed across all civilizations and time periods.

24. **FEUDALISM**—A system in western Europe and Japan in the era c. 1200–c. 1450, in which people were bound to the land and served as agricultural workers for landowners. Regional armies fought over land rights at the bidding of their local lords. In Europe, the unfree workers were called serfs, elite warriors were knights; in Japan, warriors were called samurai.

25. **ZHENG HE**—Representing the power of the Ming dynasty, the explorer Zheng He led enormous expeditions that included huge treasure ships and thousands of sailors. His fleets crossed the Indian Ocean and traveled to the Spice Islands of Southeast Asia in the early 15th century.

UNITS 3 AND 4 | LAND-BASED EMPIRES AND TRANSOCEANIC INTERCONNECTIONS, c. 1450 to c. 1750

26. **LAND-BASED EMPIRES**—In this era, many significant empires arose that were primarily connected by land, not sea. Armies used gunpowder, a Chinese invention, to expand with force. These included the Qing (Manchu) dynasty in Central and East Asia, Russia in Eastern Europe and Asia, the Mughal and Ottoman Empires (see below), and the Safavids in the Middle East.

27. **INCA AND MEXICA (AZTEC) EMPIRES**—Centered in the Andes Mountains in western South America, the Inca civilization was built on previous cultures. Their empire extended along the western coast, a result of both conquest and diplomacy. Pivotal to Incan economic strength was the mit'a system, which imposed forced labor on indigenous peoples. This system allowed for the creation of a massive mandatory public works program that made possible an extensive road network, construction of public buildings, and later, under the Spanish, mining (see entry No. 33). Its influence peaked in the 15th century but declined rapidly when Spanish conquistadors arrived in the early 16th century. Similarly, the Mexica (Aztec) empire was built upon features of earlier cultures, like the Maya, and fell after the arrival of the Spanish. Its capital was located in central Mexico.

28. **EUROPEAN EXPLORATIONS**—Seeking an increase in the trade of spices, silk, and other goods from East and Southeast Asia, kings from new European nations sent expeditions around Africa into the Indian Ocean and also across the Atlantic Ocean. Started by Portugal, then Spain, France, Britain, and the Netherlands (a.k.a. the Dutch), these explorers initiated the first truly global contacts and ushered in the rise of European influence around the world.

29. **COLUMBIAN EXCHANGE**—Columbus's expeditions to the Americas triggered exchanges of plants, animals, technology, and diseases globally. (This term is a key definition in the global scope of AP® World History: Modern.)

30. **ATLANTIC WORLD**—The Atlantic World includes the people, politics, religions, goods, and ideas that crossed back and forth on the Atlantic Ocean after Columbus's journeys connected Europe,

Africa, and North and South America. This term is especially important in the years 1450–1900.

31. **MERCANTILISM**—The west European governments of Portugal, Spain, Britain, France, and the Dutch expanded their new maritime empires into worldwide power because of the Columbian Exchange. Each established mercantilism as an example of economic nationalism. Under mercantilist policies, nations developed colonies in the Americas and Asia and used them to provide raw materials such as sugar, furs, silver, and lumber. These products were then processed and sold by companies from the owner (mercantilist) nation all over the world. Each nation competed to amass as many colonies as possible as a sign of economic and political power. Silver mining and trade were the foundation of mercantilist system.

32. **ATLANTIC SLAVE TRADE**—European mercantilists needed many workers on their large Caribbean sugar plantations. These laborers were found mainly in West Africa, where trade in humans connected the Asante (Ashanti) and Kongo kingdoms with the Atlantic World. From the 16th to the 19th centuries, millions of people were shipped across the Atlantic in the so-called middle passage. As a result, great demographic changes occurred in both Africa and the New World.

33. **ENCOMIENDA AND MIT'A SYSTEMS**—The encomienda system was a Spanish land-use practice in its American colonies and the Philippines. Spanish settlers were granted tracts of land and permitted to use the native people already living on that land as indentured servants. The mit'a system was a form of labor (e.g., road building) required by the Incan government, and adopted by the Spanish for gold mining.

34. **MUGHAL EMPIRE**—This Muslim territory in South Asia ruled from the mid-16th to the 19th centuries. One of its famous leaders was Akbar. Religious tolerance was one of its practices. The Taj Mahal was built during its reign. Mughal leaders claimed to be descended from the Mongols, from which the name "Mughal" derived.

35. **PRINTING PRESS**—Developed in China c. 500 CE, printing technology moved along trade routes, arriving in Germany by the 15th century, where it spread rapidly across Europe. The printing press helped disseminate the tenets of the Reformation and significantly changed human communication.

36. **OTTOMAN EMPIRE**—Expanding from Southwest Asia into parts of North Africa and Eastern Europe, this Muslim empire survived from the 13th century to the early 20th century. Ottoman Turks ruled this large empire, an important political, social, and economic conduit for Western Europe, Africa, and East Asia.

37. **DIASPORIC AND INDIGENOUS CULTURES**—"Diasporic" is a fancy term for "scattered." Refugees, missionaries, and merchants set up communities in faraway places, such as Jewish merchants from Southwest Asia in China. Indigenous peoples are those who were "there first," like the peoples living in Australia before Europeans arrived.

38. **URBANIZATION**—Refers to cities: their importance, growth and decline. Cities were and remain centers of government, religion, trade, education, and the arts.

UNITS 5 AND 6 | REVOLUTIONS AND CONSEQUENCES OF INDUSTRIALIZATION, c. 1750 TO c. 1900

39. **INDUSTRIALIZATION**—The Industrial Revolution began in Britain in the mid-18th century and was a major part of the West's enormous social changes and economic and political expansions in the nineteenth century. It marks the shift from slow hand-made to rapid machine-made production. Industrialization spread to Russia, South and East Asia, and North and South America by the end of the 19th century.

40. **THE ENLIGHTENMENT**—Like the Industrial Revolution, the Enlightenment was a western European development that had tremendous global impact. With foundations in scientific study and intellectual reason, its basic tenets included individual rights such as freedom of speech and participation in government. It greatly influenced the American and French Revolutions, which then inspired political revolutions around the world.

41. **CAPITALISM**—An offshoot of the Enlightenment and strongly attached to the Industrial Revolution, capitalism is an economic system based on individual economic development. Private investors use their money (capital) to invest in potentially profitable activities. Scotsman Adam Smith was an important proponent of capitalism.

The industrialized nations of the early 21st century hang their economic hats on capitalism to varying degrees.

42. **MARXISM**—In the mid-19th century, Karl Marx proposed an alternative to capitalism in an attempt to close the gap between the rich and poor in industrial western Europe and later, he hoped, the world. Marxism advocates that the many poor should unite and overthrow the few rich, and establish a political and economic system where the government controls production and labor to benefit the masses.

43. **NATIONALISM**—The belief that people with similar cultural backgrounds rightly belong together in one nation. It became popular in western Europe in the 19th century and spread globally, leading to many wars for independence, most notably in Latin America, and against Ottoman and Austrian rule in Eastern Europe.

44. **LIBERALISM**—Inspired by the Enlightenment in the 19th century, this political philosophy called for written constitutions, increased voting rights, equality for all and economic freedom. It fueled many revolutions in the Americas and Europe.

45. **AGE OF REVOLUTIONS**—During the mid-19th-century "Age of Isms" in western Europe (see entry Nos. 41 through 44), many revolutions seeking political and social change occurred, inspired by the ideas of the Enlightenment and the French Revolution. In Latin America, most countries successfully revolted against European political control.

46. **IMPERIALISM**—In the 19th century, western Europe's economic and industrial power made it the world's strongest political force, and its nations accumulated colonies all over the world. Russia, Japan, and the U.S. also participated. A famous quotation that reflects the national pride that accompanied imperialist expansion was, "The sun never sets on the British Empire." At its peak, Britain claimed colonies in half of Africa and much of South and Southeast Asia.

47. **SOCIAL DARWINISM**—Connected to strong nationalist ideas, Europe's political and industrial superiority led to the belief that it was socially and morally superior to the peoples it conquered. Charles Darwin's "survival of the fittest" scientific theory in the animal world was applied to non-European peoples around the globe.

48. RESISTANCE TO WESTERN HEGEMONY—"Hegemony" is dominance or control. Resistance in Asia and Africa to European imperialism was widespread. For example, the Chinese tried to stop Britain's importation of opium; anti-colonial rebellions broke out in Africa; and in India, the National Congress promoted self-rule.

49. MEIJI RESTORATION—To compete with the West's industrial and political power, Japan embarked upon the Meiji Restoration, reorganizing its government in the late 19th century. The emperor's power was reestablished, and Japan westernized its industrial base and its society.

50. 19TH-CENTURY MIGRATIONS—The Industrial Revolution included improvements in transportation that made ocean travel safer and cheaper. Pushed by revolutions and poor living conditions, and pulled by stories of opportunities, millions—especially Europeans but also South and East Asians—migrated to North and South America in the 19th century.

51. INDENTURED SERVITUDE—A form of coercive labor where a person exchanges his or her work for a period of time—usually a few years—for transportation and necessities, without other pay. After the term of indenture was completed, the laborer was supposed to be freed. Indentured servitude was a factor in migrations to the Americas in the 17th and 18th centuries, but was replaced by slavery. By the end of the 19th century, slavery in the West had ended and indentured servitude returned. In that era, thousands of South Asians migrated to South Africa and the Caribbean as agricultural indentured servants. East Asians were also employed as indentured servants in the Americas.

52. OPEN DOOR POLICY—In the early 20th century, the U.S. flexed its new global muscles by gaining approval for a plan that the U.S., Japan, and the European powers shared open access to trade with China. The weak Chinese government could not resist the economic and political pressure of these nations. The Open Door Policy was a sign of the "arrival" of the U.S. in global affairs.

53. "SECOND" INDUSTRIAL REVOLUTION—The "first" Industrial Revolution involved the mechanization of agriculture and textiles, but in the last half of the 19th century, its focus changed to innovations in electricity (telephone and radio), chemistry (fertilizers), transportation (cars and airplanes), and steel (skyscrapers and modern weapons). These developments continued to influence the rapid social and economic changes in the West into the 20th century.

UNITS 7, 8, AND 9 | GLOBAL CONFLICT, COLD WAR AND DECOLONIZATION, AND GLOBALIZATION, c. 1900 TO THE PRESENT

54. **THE WORLD WARS**—The first half of the 20th century saw two enormous wars among the "Great Powers" of Europe, Asia, and the U.S. One cause was the massive military production made possible by the Industrial Revolution and by global competition for territories during the Age of Imperialism. In an AP® World History: Modern context, World Wars I and II can be seen as one long global war with a 20-year break between the two. The results of the wars were the decline of western Europe and the rise of the power of the U.S. and Soviet Union in the second half of the 20th century.

55. **THE GREAT DEPRESSION**—Between the two World Wars, a global economic disaster struck the industrialized nations around the world. After World War I, the U.S. had the world's largest economy; when it failed in the late 1920s, the economies of much of the rest of the world, already reeling from the effects of World War I, were severely affected. Two major results were the rise of authoritarian governments (see entry No. 56) and the outbreak of World War II.

56. **AUTHORITARIANISM**—One result of the catastrophe of World War I was a rejection of democratic forms of government in parts of Europe and Asia, namely, Germany, Italy, Russia, and Japan. Single-party rule led by a strongman with dictatorial powers was thought to be a more efficient system than democracy. Communism and fascism were the best-known examples of such governmental systems. The growing military aggression of the fascist governments was a cause of World War II.

57. **COMMUNISM**—Communism was originally proposed by Karl Marx from Germany in the mid-19th century and put in place by Vladimir Lenin in Russia in the early 20th century. In this economic and political system of socialism, the government (the state)

directs the economy (e.g., the Soviet Union's Five-Year Plans) and promises to provide services for all. Authoritarianism was often the method of rule in communist systems. Communism spread around the globe in the 20th century and competed directly with capitalist societies.

58. **DECOLONIZATION**—A major global development after World War II was the end of Europe's colonial empires around the world. Colonies in South Asia, Southeast Asia, and Africa regained their independence some peacefully, others through violence. The new independent states often faced significant social, economic, and political challenges.

59. **PARTITION**—The largest British colony, India, partitioned (split up) itself along religious lines when it gained independence in 1947, forming India (with a Hindu majority) and Pakistan. In 1971, East Pakistan separated from Pakistan to become Bangladesh (both with Muslim majorities). For many decades afterward, Pakistan and India were major rivals in South Asia.

60. **COLD WAR**—The dominant global conflict after World War II, the Cold War was conducted between the U.S. (and its allies) and the Soviet Union (and its allies). The aim for each side was to keep the other from increasing its political and economic influence globally. It was called the Cold War because the two sides did everything to prepare for a real "hot" war (with real weapons) except actually fight each other directly. This led to proxy wars like the Korean War, the Angolan Civil War, and the Sandinista-Contras Conflict in Nicaragua. Massive accumulation of nuclear and other forms of weapons threatened mutually assured destruction, but when the Soviet Union fell apart in the late 20th century, the Cold War ended.

61. **MULTINATIONAL OR TRANSNATIONAL CORPORATIONS**—A multinational or transnational corporation does business in more than one country. The British and Dutch East India companies of the 18th century were early examples, but it was after World War II that this business model became common. Today, Exxon Mobil, Toyota, and General Electric are prominent multinational corporations.

62. **PACIFIC RIM**—In the second half of the 20th century, strong economies developed on both sides of the Pacific. Although the U.S. was a major economic power in the region, the term usually refers to the economies based in nations such as China, Japan, Australia, South Korea, and Singapore.

63. **CHINESE REVOLUTIONS**—In the early 20th century, a revolution in China against the emperor led to a limited democracy. After World War II, communists led by Mao Zedong overthrew that government. Vast social, political, and economic changes resulted as the government took control of the national economy through the Great Leap Forward in 1958. The result was to choke the economy and cause millions of deaths from starvation, execution, torture, forced labor, and suicide. Until the late 20th century, communist China was relatively isolated from global economic involvement, but after Mao's death, China opened its economic system to allow capitalist development, and its economy boomed.

64. **APARTHEID**—Apartheid was a political and social policy in South Africa in the mid-20th century that separated whites and blacks and that granted the white minority many rights that the black majority was denied. The apartheid policy was reversed in the late 20th century after decades of global pressure, and majority rule was established.

65. **FEMINISM**—Although its roots extended back to the Enlightenment (see entry No. 40), feminism was largely a 20th-century movement dedicated to increasing the political, social, and economic rights of women. It began in Western democracies and expanded to include much of the world by century's end. Counterexamples persisted in parts of the Middle East, Africa, and Asia.

66. **GLOBALIZATION**—"Globalization" describes the "shrinking world" that resulted from increased economic and communications connections. While the term *could* be applied to world systems after Columbus's voyages (see entry No. 29) or to the Age of Imperialism (see entry No. 46), it became especially popular in the late 20th century. Not everyone was content with the process of globalization.

World Regions in AP® World History

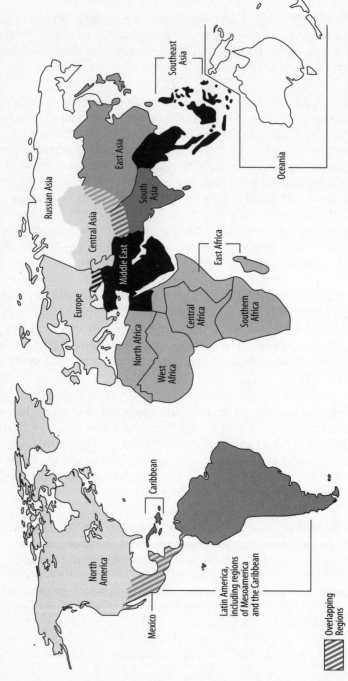

North America

Mexico

Caribbean

Latin America, including regions of Mesoamerica and the Caribbean

Europe

Russian Asia

Central Asia

Middle East

North Africa

West Africa

Central Africa

East Africa

Southern Africa

South Asia

East Asia

Southeast Asia

Oceania

Overlapping Regions

Map copyright © 2019 the College Board.

This map shows significant subregions within the five major geographical regions.

AP® World History: Modern Course Overview

Below is the outline based on the College Board's released units of the entire AP® World History: Modern course. Studying this will help you form the "big picture" of the last eight hundred years of history. The course is divided into 9 units that contain sub-topics with further details. After this outline, Chapters 4 through 12 contain a more detailed chronological review of the events, processes, and connections to best prepare you for the exam.

Build your knowledge by writing down features and the significance for each topic. For example, consider the Columbian Exchange (4.3). Define the exchange and list some elements:

To the Americas: horses, pigs, cows, sugar cane, African slavery.

From the Americas: potatoes, corn, silver.

Created first truly global trade network, set up Atlantic World.

UNITS 1 AND 2 | c. 1200 to c. 1450 (16%–20% of the exam)

Unit 1: The Global Tapestry

1.1 Developments in East Asia from c. 1200 to c. 1450

1.2 Developments in Dar al-Islam from c. 1200 to c. 1450

1.3 Developments in South and Southeast Asia from c. 1200 to c. 1450

1.4 State Building in the Americas

1.5 State Building in Africa

1.6 Developments in Europe from c. 1200 to c. 1450

1.7 Comparison in the Period from c. 1200 to c. 1450

Unit 2: Networks of Exchange

    2.1 The Silk Roads

    2.2 The Mongol Empire and the Making of the Modern World

    2.3 Exchange in the Indian Ocean

    2.4 Trans-Saharan Trade Routes

    2.5 Cultural Consequences of Connectivity

    2.6 Environmental Consequences of Connectivity

    2.7 Comparison of Economic Exchange

UNITS 3 AND 4 | c. 1450 to c. 1750 (24%–30% of the exam)

Unit 3: Land-Based Empires

    3.1 Empires Expand

    3.2 Empires: Administration

    3.3 Empires: Belief Systems

    3.4 Comparison in Land-Based Empires

Unit 4: Transoceanic Interconnections

    4.1 Technological Innovations from 1450 to 1750

    4.2 Exploration: Causes and Events from 1450 to 1750

    4.3 Columbian Exchange

    4.4 Maritime Empires Established

    4.5 Maritime Empires Maintained and Developed

    4.6 Internal and External Challenges to State Power from 1450 to 1750

    4.7 Changing Social Hierarchies from 1450 to 1750

    4.8 Continuity and Change from 1450 to 1750

UNITS 5 AND 6 | c. 1750 to c. 1900
(24%–30% of the exam)

Unit 5: Revolutions

5.1 The Enlightenment

5.2 Nationalism and Revolutions in the Period from 1750 to 1900

5.3 Industrial Revolution Begins

5.4 Industrialization Spreads in the Period from 1750 to 1900

5.5 Technology of the Industrial Age

5.6 Industrialization: Government's Role from 1750 to 1900

5.7 Economic Developments and Innovations in the Industrial Age

5.8 Reactions to the Industrial Economy from 1750 to 1900

5.9 Society and the Industrial Age

5.10 Continuity and Change in the Industrial Age

Unit 6: Consequences of Industrialization

6.1 Rationales for Imperialism from 1750 to 1900

6.2 State Expansion from 1750 to 1900

6.3 Indigenous Responses to State Expansion from 1750 to 1900

6.4 Global Economic Development from 1750 to 1900

6.5 Economic Imperialism from 1750 to 1900

6.6 Causes of Migrations in an Interconnected World

6.7 Effects of Migrations

6.8 Causation in the Imperial Age

UNITS 7, 8, AND 9 | c. 1900 to the Present
(24%–30% of the exam)

Unit 7: Global Conflict

7.1 Shifting Power After 1900

7.2 Causes of World War I

PART II

CHRONOLOGICAL REVIEW

UNIT 1 | The Global Tapestry
c. 1200 to c. 1450

The first unit in AP® World History: Modern covers developments from c. 1200 CE to c. 1450 CE, and focuses on processes involving governments and cultures.

For the exam, the term *governments* means more than just what kings did. Think connections. Governments promoted and resisted religions and the arts, depending on the point of view of the leaders, but they all usually encouraged trade and technology. And of course, all governments tried to retain power.

Political and social trends from before this era greatly influenced later generations, including societies today. Spurred by the increase in trade, religions continued to spread over a wide area in this era, creating long-term effects in places far from their points of origin. Faith offered comfort in difficult times, created social stability and structure, and provided authority to political leaders.

 I. DEVELOPMENTS IN EAST ASIA (c. 1200 to c. 1450)

A. SPREAD OF CHINESE CULTURAL TRADITIONS

1. Confucianism and filial piety continued. The teachings of Confucius are fundamentally about maintaining order in society, even in times of political chaos, such as after the fall of a dynasty. Filial piety is the unquestioned respect for the family's father. He in turn respects his superiors, who respect theirs, all the way up to the emperor. If everybody "knows their place" (think of Mulan) in this highly patriarchal society, it will continue through good and bad times. Confucianism did not promise a heavenly reward for following these rules, but was a philosophy for *this* life.

2. Buddhism originated in India and spread to China along the Silk Roads. As it spread, it changed to fit local conditions, something all major religions do. The original form, Theravada Buddhism, was less popular in East Asia than Mahayana Buddhism, which emphasizes more hope for eternal life.

3. By 1200, Neo-Confucianism had become popular in China. It blended concepts from Buddhism, the ancient Chinese Daoist beliefs, and Confucianism into one, making Neo-Confucianism more of a religion than only a philosophy.

4. Foot binding of women's feet regained popularity and continued into the early 20th century. Historians say foot binding was another sign of Confucian patriarchy.

5. Diasporic communities, consisting of Christians, Jews, and Muslims, grew in China. These groups arrived along trade routes, becoming merchants and government officials and assuming roles necessary to establish nodes of commerce and state-sponsored commercial infrastructure.

6. Confucianism, Neo-Confucianism, and forms of Buddhism spread to Korea, Heian Japan, and Vietnam and greatly influenced those countries' cultures, including their leaders.

7. Chinese forms of government, literature, and art spread to Korea, Heian Japan, and Vietnam during this era.

B. SONG DYNASTY, CHINA (960–1279)

1. China had the most advanced civilization in the world: the largest cities, the strongest economy, and the latest technologies. Kaifeng and Hangzhou were prosperous trade and government centers, each with at least a million residents.

2. China's economy soared based on massive exports to East Africa, Arabia, and South and Southeast Asia. Chinese craftsmen produced exquisite porcelain ("china"), iron and steel, and, of course, tea and silk.

3. The greatest boon to agriculture was the introduction of fast-growing Champa rice from Vietnam. This new crop provided for a rapidly expanding population.

4. China invented paper money during this era and had a policy of taxing all imports, sometimes at very high rates.

5. Technology advanced during the Song dynasty. Gunpowder, wood block printing, the compass, and an expanded Grand Canal are just some of the many inventions and innovations developed by the Song civilization.

II. DEVELOPMENTS IN DAR AL-ISLAM (c. 1200 to c. 1450)

A. INFLUENCE OF ISLAM, JUDAISM, AND CHRISTIANITY IN AFRICA AND ASIA

1. Islam originated in Arabia in the 7th century and expanded rapidly west across North Africa into Spain and West Africa, north into Turkey, south along the east coast of Africa (the Swahili states), and east into South and Central Asia, both peacefully and by force. Islam saw several political changes in the era c. 1200–c. 1450. See below.

2. Christianity retreated in the region of Turkey, supplanted by Islam, but gained in Spain, reasserting its dominance over Islam by c. 1450.

3. Jews lived in scattered communities throughout Afro-Eurasia ("the diaspora"). Merchants, scholars, artisans, and government officials were some jobs Jews held. Sadly, however, with acceptance came persecution. Countries in Europe sought to expel Jews in this era, sometimes out of religious rivalry and other times out of fear that Jews were somehow responsible for the Black Death.

B. NEW ISLAMIC POLITICAL STATES

1. The Abbasid caliphate (i.e., a Muslim political state under religious rule) began declining before c. 1200 and then fell when Mongols sacked the capital city of Baghdad in 1258. Other Muslim governments rose in this era.

2. The Mamluks were a professional army established by the Abbasids. The Mamluks later set up a sultanate (region headed by a Muslim ruler) in Egypt. They also moved into Central Asia and established the Delhi Sultanate, which ruled much of South Asia, and repelled Mongol invasions.

3. As the Abbasids declined, Turkish groups from Central Asia moved into Southwest Asia and formed the Muslim Ottoman Empire in Turkey in the late 13th century and rapidly expanded.

4. Sufism, a mystical form of Islam, grew along with the new governments, ranging from Eastern Europe to North Africa into Central and South Asia.

C. MUSLIM ADVANCES IN TECHNOLOGY AND SCIENCE

1. Muslim scholars were among the world's leaders in medicine and astronomy. They preserved Greek and Roman literature and made several advances in mathematics during this era.

2. The most famous example of Muslim scholarship was the Abbasid Empire's "House of Wisdom" in Baghdad, a center of philosophy, science, and engineering that was destroyed in the Mongol invasion of 1258.

3. Cultural transfers in Muslim and Christian Spain included mathematics and knowledge of Greek and Roman literature, which had been preserved by Muslim scholars.

III. SOUTH AND SOUTHEAST ASIA (c. 1200 to c. 1450)

A. HINDUISM, ISLAM, AND BUDDHISM SHAPED SOCIETIES

1. The Bhakti movement in Hinduism became popular in South Asia. It marked a shift in devotion to a personal god. Some historians believe this movement was a response to the growing influence of Islam in South Asia at this time.

2. As referenced above, Sufism in Islam rapidly expanded in South and Central Asia. Native Islamic sultanates were established in Sumatra by the 15th and 16th centuries. The trade city of Malacca was also a center of Islam and a major conduit for the spread of the faith in Southeast Asia.

B. NEW HINDU AND BUDDHIST STATES

1. The Vijayanagara Empire was a Hindu-led state that arose in the southern half of South Asia, as a counter to Muslim expansion

to the north. At the same time, smaller Hindu states, the Rajput kingdoms, occupied parts of South Asia.

2. Meanwhile, the Buddhist Srivijaya Empire in Southeast Asia, which had dominated trade there for centuries, was conquered in the late 1200s.

IV. STATE BUILDING IN THE AMERICAS (c. 1200 to c. 1450)

A. AS IN AFRO-EURASIA, STATES CONTINUED AND DEVELOPED IN THE AMERICAS

1. The best known states in the era c. 1200 to c. 1450 were the Mayan city-states, Mexica (the Aztecs), the Inca Empire, and Cahokia. Note that the AP® exam considers the Maya an illustrative example of the period even though the once-powerful Mayan city-states, based in what is today's Mexico, had been abandoned by 900 CE.

2. In Central Mexico, many aspects of the Toltec culture, like religion and architecture, were adopted by the Mexica, also known as the Aztecs. Their king was considered to be a god.

3. The Mexica had an extensive empire in central Mexico, with Tenochtitlan as its capital. The empire grew through conquest of neighbors whom they ruled indirectly via a tribute system.

4. The Incas had an enormous empire that ran along the west coast of South America, primarily along the Andes Mountains. Their most famous features were extensive road and bridge systems and a government-controlled distribution system of goods and agriculture. As in the Mexica Empire, their king was considered divine.

5. Cahokia was located near today's St. Louis, Missouri. It was a complex of buildings and earthen mounds from the Mississippian culture. Cahokia was a major trade and religious center. The Cahokian people used the Mississippi River to conduct long-distance trade as far as the Gulf of Mexico. They were effective urban planners and farmers, but lacked a writing system.

V. STATE BUILDING IN AFRICA (c. 1200 to c. 1450)

A. EMERGENCE OF TWO EMPIRES

1. Great Zimbabwe was a major civilization in southeast Africa. It featured impressive stone buildings and flourishing trade. Great Zimbabwe traded directly with social groups in the interior of Africa and with cities along the Swahili Coast, such as Kilwa. There is also evidence they traded indirectly with South Asia and China.

2. Ethiopia was an empire in the northern part of East Africa led by dynasties of Christian kings, who sought help from European Christian rulers to fight Muslim incursions into the empire. Ethiopia was a major cultural and economic crossroads in the region. Its most famous feature is the "rock churches" built during the reign of the Emperor Lalibela.

VI. DEVELOPMENTS IN EUROPE (c. 1200 to c. 1450)

A. EUROPE FRAGMENTED POLITICALLY AND RELIGIOUSLY

1. The pandemic bubonic plague known as the Black Death in Afro-Eurasia in the 14th century hit Western Europe the hardest. The political and cultural power of the Catholic Church in Western Europe was weakened.

2. The feudal system of lords, manors, and serfs began to break down, leading to the freeing of serfs by c. 1500.

3. Historically, Europe was similar to South Asia in that it had rarely been unified under one government.

4. The Hundred Years War between Britain and France contributed to the fall of feudalism, and strengthened the rise of a single monarch in each country.

5. The Holy Roman Empire in Central Europe continued as a loose union of several small kingdoms. Italy was politically fragmented as well.

B. RELIGIOUS FRAGMENTATION EXPANDED IN EUROPE

1. While the Catholic Church lost prestige and power in the rest of Western Europe, in Portugal and Spain the "Reconquista"

of Catholicism over Islam continued and was completed just before 1500.

2. Although Islam lost ground in Spain and Portugal, its influence increased in Eastern Europe. Orthodox Christianity, which split from Roman Catholicism in the 11th century, remained predominant.

> *Be prepared to compare (similarities and differences) the processes of the development, maintenance, and decline of states in this era (c. 1200 to c. 1450). For example: To what extent were leaders in the Americas and China similar in the ways they used religion to justify their rule? To what extent was the spread of Christianity and Islam similar in this era?*

Origins and Diffusion Routes for Selected Religions to c. 1200 (Christianity, Islam, Hinduism, and Buddhism)

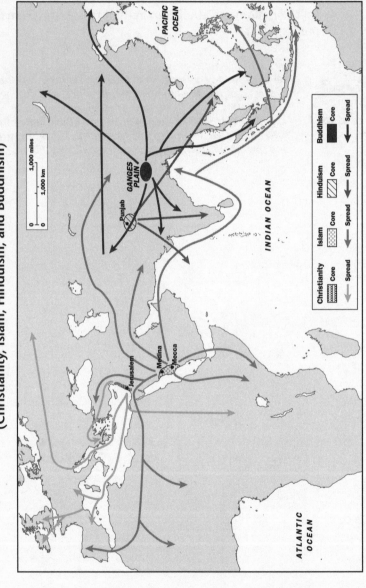

UNIT
2
Networks of Exchange
c. 1200 to c. 1450

Connected to the political and religious processes c. 1200–c.1450 are the economic and social changes and continuities in the world. But you will discover politics, religions, and philosophies here too. This is a good reminder of the constant overlapping of historical events and trends that make AP® World History: Modern special. As you proceed through this book, remember to continually apply the AP® skills: Comparison (similarities and differences), Continuity-and-Change-over-Time, and Causes and Effects. As you review these chapters, think, "How is this similar or different from another society?" "What caused this?" "What are some of its effects?" "What things are changing?" "What things are staying much the same?"

 I. **THE SILK ROADS**

A. TRADE CITIES AND INNOVATIONS

1. The Silk Roads existed long before 1200, but were longer and busier than ever, running from Korea to the Mediterranean Sea.

2. The increase in trade that took place along the Silk Roads led to stopping points (called *caravanserai*) along the routes. Some caravanserai developed into cities that expanded in importance in this era. Samarkand and Dunhuang are two examples of Silk Road trade cities.

   i. These cities were centers for exchanging goods like silk textiles, porcelain and tea from China, amber from the Black Sea region, carpets and musical instruments from Central Asia, spices from South and Southeast Asia, and the gold and silver from faraway Europe.

   ii. Technology and other ideas were also exchanged, such as gunpowder, paper, and the compass from China, and Arabic numerals from South Asia.

iii. Merchants and missionaries spread Islam, Buddhism, and Christianity as well as other faiths along trade routes.

B. NEW FORMS OF MONEY AND CREDIT

1. Banks grew along the Silk Roads. They provided bills of exchange (like today's bank-issued checks) to protect merchants' money.

2. China's exports were so strong, paper money ("flying cash") was introduced as currency due to a shortage of metal for coins. The innovation grew in popularity along the Silk Roads after the Mongols conquered China.

II. MONGOL EMPIRE AND MAKING OF THE MODERN WORLD

A. FROM THE 13th TO THE 15th CENTURIES, MONGOL RULE STRETCHED FROM EAST ASIA TO EASTERN EUROPE

1. The Mongols were pastoralists—nomads from Mongolia who herded sheep, yaks, goats, cattle, and, most importantly, horses. In the early 13th century, led by Chinggis (Genghis) Khan, the Mongols swept south into China, eventually reaching—and ending—the Song Dynasty.

2. After merciless military campaigns that brought them to power, the Mongols in China made Beijing their capital and ended the Confucian examination system. The Mongols allowed foreigners, especially Arab Muslims, to administer the government.

3. Chinggis's grandson, Kublai Khan, established the Yuan Dynasty in China, which lasted until 1368, when rebellions drove the Mongols back to their homeland on the steppes of Mongolia.

B. THE PAX MONGOLICA

1. The Mongols accumulated goods from all over the world, so they made the Silk Road network as safe for merchants as possible. The routes were so free of bandits that historians refer to a Pax Mongolica ("Mongol peace").

2. The Pax Mongolica came at a high price: cities that opposed the Mongols disappeared from the map; Baghdad's leaders resisted Mongol attacks in 1258 and 200,000 people died. The Abbasid Empire died with them. Central Asia lost as many as three-quarters of its population to Mongol destruction. It is estimated that China's population declined by half during the Yuan Dynasty.

C. MONGOL EXPANSION

1. Through conquest, the Mongol Empire grew so quickly that one leader could not oversee it all. The Empire divided into regional *khanates* after Chinggis died, and these khanates reached to eastern Europe, Central Asia, and Southwest Asia.

2. The Mongols' advance westward was finally stopped in modern-day Israel by Mamluk warriors from Egypt.

3. The Russians called the Mongols "The Golden Horde." After their destructive invasion, the Mongols reached an agreement with local Russian leaders who collected tribute to send to their Mongol masters. This tribute arrangement lasted 200 years until Ivan the Great, prince of Moscow, led a successful revolt against the Mongols in 1480.

4. The Mongols established a tribute system of trade with Korea, but failed twice to invade Japan by sea.

D. EFFECTS OF THE MONGOLS

1. Over time, the people in all Mongol khanates rebelled and ended their rule. But the Mongol legacy, the largest empire the world has ever seen, remained. They allowed freedom of religion in the areas they conquered. Technology and other innovations spread through the Mongol Empire and beyond: saddle stirrups, the compound bow, flying cash, and pasta, to name a few.

2. Marco Polo returned to Italy from a long visit to China under Kublai Khan with noodle-making technology and enticing tales that inspired future generations of European explorers. However, because of the Pax Mongolica, increased trade resulted in the rapid spread of the Black Death all across the khanates and into western Europe. Mongols in Persia even settled down to become farmers!

UNIT 2 | c. 1200 to c. 1450

III. EXCHANGE IN THE INDIAN OCEAN

A. EXPANSION OF INTERREGIONAL TRADE

1. Similar to the Silk Roads, the Indian Ocean trade network was just as important but with routes over water.

2. Ships carried heavier bulk items (lumber and pottery) than could be conveyed on the Silk Roads. Bananas and citrus trees from Southeast Asia were cultivated in Africa and around the Mediterranean region. African, Arab, Southeast Asian, and Chinese (just to name a few!) merchants also carried religion (especially Buddhism and Islam) and exchanged silver, cotton, spices, porcelain, and many other items across the Indian Ocean.

   i. Seasonal monsoon winds aided sailing ships in the Indian Ocean. Merchants entered Southeast Asia, crossing the Indian Ocean into South Asia, East Africa, and the Middle East (which is part of Southwest Asia).

   ii. China ruled the seas from East Africa to East Asia. Chinese emperors usually let the Indian Ocean merchants manage their own affairs. Therefore, the Indian Ocean system of exchange was mostly self-governing. Merchants made the rules, worked their best deals for access to ports, kept smugglers (pirates) at bay, and established prices.

   iii. The introduction of the compass, the astrolabe, and larger ships made trade safer and profitable.

   iv. History's greatest maritime expeditions passed through the Indian Ocean. In the early 15th century, the Ming Dynasty sent a huge fleet to the Indian Ocean led by Chinese Muslim Admiral Zheng He for an official look at its sea-trading partners. His seven voyages on 400-foot-long "treasure ships" displayed China's vast wealth, technology, and power.

B. INDIAN OCEAN TRADE AND GROWTH OF STATES

1. The Islamic Sultanate of Malacca, in Southeast Asia, was a major player in Indian Ocean trade. It patrolled the vital Straits of Malacca (a route from China to the Indian Ocean) for pirates.

2. In western India, the port of Gujarat, under Islamic control, was a trade center midway between Africa and East Asia.

3. Muslims also controlled the trading centers on the Swahili Coast of East Africa. Cities such as Kilwa, Lamu, and Zanzibar welcomed various merchants from Europe, the Arabian Peninsula, South Asia, Southeast Asia, and East Asia.

4. All this merchant activity meant there were sizable diasporic communities scattered all over Afro-Eurasia, especially Arabs and Persians in East Africa, Chinese in Southeast Asia (like Burma and modern-day Indonesia) and Malays in South Asia.

5. Jewish and Christian merchants also participated in the Indian Ocean network and established communities throughout the region.

IV. TRANS-SAHARAN TRADE ROUTES

A. SAHARA TRADE RELIANCE ON NEW TRANSPORTATION TECHNOLOGIES

1. South of the "rim" of Mediterranean North Africa lies the Sahara Desert. Merchants there exchanged items from the coast such as cotton, dates, and leather goods for gold, salt, ivory, animal hides, and slaves, connecting to the Silk Road network.

2. Camels were introduced to the Sahara from the Middle East centuries before 1200.

   i. Camels became the main means to transport goods, greatly increasing trade between West Africa and Southwest Asia.

   ii. The camel saddle and use of camel caravans encouraged trade across the Sahara, into Southwest Asia, all the way to China and Korea.

3. Islam was introduced into the region in the eighth century along the trans-Sahara trade routes, just as Buddhism had earlier spread into East and Southeast Asia.

B. WEST AFRICAN KINGDOMS IN TRANS-SAHARAN TRADE

1. The Muslim West African kingdom of Mali increased Afro-Eurasian trade, exchanging its gold and animal skins for goods from beyond its borders, including salt.

    i. Its capital, Timbuktu, was a major trade, religious, and educational center.

    ii. Mali's king Mansa Musa made a famous pilgrimage to the Islamic holy city, Mecca.

    iii. Famous Muslim traveler, Ibn Battuta recorded a visit to Mali (and the Swahili Coast, Central, South, Southeast and East Asia) in the 14th century.

2. Songhai, a similar empire, appeared late in this era and competed with Mali for trade dominance. The trade center Gao was its capital.

Test Tip

Practice writing cause-and-effect essays about how cultures responded to the many outside influences that long-distance trade brought. For example, "To what extent did the exchange of innovations (new technology, ideas or goods) affect cultures along the Silk Roads?"

Note the most common environmental question related to trade routes is negative: the spread of the bubonic plague (Black Death).

Here's a practice question:

> *To what extent did the expansion of trade in Afro-Eurasia during the Mongol Empire increase the number of fatalities from the bubonic plague?*

Here's another:

> *To what extent did the Mongols' culture change after they established empires in East Asia and Central Asia?*

V. COMPARISON OF ECONOMIC EXCHANGES

The AP® World History: Modern exam often compares features of the Silk Roads, the Indian Ocean network, and the Trans-Saharan trade routes. For example: "Analyze the extent to which the kinds of goods exchanged were similar in the Indian Ocean and the Trans-Saharan trade routes." Or, "To what extent did networks of exchange in the era c. 1200 to c. 1450 foster change in local economies?"

UNIT 3
Land-Based Empires
c. 1450 to c. 1750

Many students think of the era c. 1450–c. 1750 as when "Columbus sailed the ocean blue" and brought the Americas into contact with Europe. Although true, the AP® World History: Modern course also discusses empires that expanded without sailing to the New World. This chapter examines features of Afro-Eurasian empires that were land-based, that is, they expanded across vast areas of forests, deserts, and grasslands. In East Asia, the Ming Dynasty in China was replaced by outsiders, the Manchu, who expanded their borders. The Ottoman Empire had been expanding since the 13th century and continued to do so into this era. The Mughals spread into South and Central Asia. Russia, which was centered in Eastern Europe, added thousands of miles of land in Asia to its empire. The Persian Safavid Empire clashed with the Ottomans and Mughals as they tried to stretch their borders.

I. EMPIRES EXPAND

Land-based empires used the Chinese innovation of gunpowder with military forces to expand, so some historians label them "gunpowder empires."

A. In China, the once-powerful Ming Dynasty weakened and was replaced by the Manchu (Qing) Dynasty, 1644–1912. The Manchus came from north of China, namely, Manchuria. They remained a minority ethnic group in the land they ruled, and adopted the Chinese language, Confucian philosophy, the Chinese bureaucracy, and continued the ancient concept of the Mandate of Heaven, which justified the rule of an emperor as long as he led the people correctly.

    1. Because they were a minority in China and outsiders, the Qing rewarded ethnic Chinese soldiers and generals who supported

their rule. They also allowed local Chinese rulers to keep their status, as long as they obeyed Qing policies.

2. The Qing were also tolerant of local faiths and customs.

B. THE OTTOMAN EMPIRE WAS ESTABLISHED IN ANATOLIA (TURKEY) AT THE END OF THE 13th CENTURY

1. The Ottoman Empire reached its peak of power during this era. The empire stretched across North Africa into Southwest Asia and north into modern Turkey, reaching almost to modern Austria. The Ottomans defeated what was left of the Byzantine Empire when they took Constantinople in 1453, renamed it Istanbul, and continued westward into Eastern Europe. Geographically and culturally it was a bridge between Europe, Africa, and Asia, encompassing Christian, Jewish, and Muslim faiths.

2. The Ottomans reached the limit of their expansion into Europe by failing to conquer Vienna, Austria, in the early 16th century and again in the late 17th century. Like Russia, the Ottoman Empire struggled with its political identity as part-Asian and part-European. Despite its history of battles with Christian Europe, it wanted to be part of the European diplomatic sphere.

3. Many Western Christians believed Muslims wanted to conquer all of Europe, especially after the Ottomans seized Constantinople in 1453.

    i. This concern for the fate of Christianity was a motivation in spreading the faith to the Americas after Columbus's discoveries.

    ii. Another factor was the European fear that trade routes through Constantinople would be cut off by the Ottomans. Thus, the search for alternate routes to the "East" began.

C. IN CENTRAL AND SOUTH ASIA IN THE EARLY 16th CENTURY, MUSLIMS FROM CENTRAL ASIA ESTABLISHED THE MUGHAL EMPIRE

1. The Mughal claimed to be descended from the Mongol ruler Chinggis Khan ("Mughal" comes from the word "Mongol").

2. Rare in Indian history, most of South Asia was united under a single government—for a while.

3. The Mughal's greatest ruler was Akbar in the 16th century. His main legacy was extending religious toleration to the 75% of the population that was Hindu.

4. Like the Ottomans, the Mughals were Muslim rulers of an empire. Unlike the Ottomans, the Mughals' faith was in the minority in their own empire. One of the world's most iconic buildings, the Taj Mahal, was built by a Muslim in the heart of Hindu territory.

D. RUSSIA BUILT THE LARGEST LAND EMPIRE OF THIS ERA, FIRST TO THE EAST ACROSS SIBERIA, THEN TO THE SOUTH AND WEST

1. Russia's entry into world affairs began with Ivan the Great, who expelled the last of the Mongol rulers in the late 15th century.

2. In the 16th century, Ivan the Terrible began a conquest of Siberia that continued for one hundred years.

3. In the early 18th century, Peter the Great fought the Ottoman, Safavid, and Swedish empires for territories.

   i. Russian migrants flocked to these areas, greatly changing the cultural make-up of these regions.

   ii. Like China, Russia generally maintained a policy of religious toleration in the regions it conquered—except for Jews.

4. Starting in the late 17th century and continuing through the late 18th century, Peter the Great and, later, Catherine the Great pushed a modernization program in Russia to bring their nation closer to the level of Western European technology and culture. This included moving the capital from Moscow to St. Petersburg, the "window on the West."

E. SAFAVID EMPIRE

1. The Safavid Empire in Persia (modern Iran) in the early 16th century sought to expand its borders by waging war with the Ottomans to the west and with the Mughals to the east.

2. Although all three of the bordering states were primarily Muslim, rivalries between factions within Islam was a significant cause of these wars.

II. EMPIRES: ADMINISTRATION

Every government uses people, money, symbols, and traditions to gain and maintain power.

A. USING ADMINISTRATIVE PROFESSIONALS TO RUN THE EMPIRE

1. Historically, rulers have used various methods to retain power. The Ottoman Empire began in the 13th century and expanded dramatically in this era.

   i. Although its Muslim leaders did not require Christians and Jews to convert to Islam, they did demand that boys in non-Muslim families in Southern Europe become soldiers.

   ii. "Recruits" were known as *Janissaries* and their "recruitment" was called the *devshirme* system. Janissaries were trained in Islam and although they were not Turks, they could be promoted by showing loyalty and ability—and many did. Sometimes the hope of upward mobility was so strong that Christian parents volunteered their sons for Janissary duty.

2. In Japan, the Tokugawa Shogunate elevated many *samurai* (feudal knights) to administrative positions in the government. Many *samurai* became artists, scholars, and poets.

B. USING RELIGION, ART, AND ARCHITECTURE TO MAINTAIN POWER

1. The Mexica (Aztec) practiced human sacrifice to appease the gods and their god/king in power.

2. European monarchs claimed the "divine right" to legitimize their power. This meant the kings believed God was on their side, so if you opposed the king, you opposed God.

3. The Songhai rulers in West Africa, the Ottomans, the Mughals and the Safavids openly practiced and promoted Islam.

4. Many monarchs around the globe commissioned (paid for) portraits of themselves, usually wearing royal robes and surrounded with other symbols of power.

5. The Inca built the famous Temple of the Sun as a monument to their religion and their king's power.

6. Monarchs impressed their rivals and supporters with large, expensive palaces like Versailles in France, the Forbidden City in China, and mausoleums like the Taj Mahal in South Asia.

C. USING TAXES TO MAINTAIN AND BUILD POWER

1. Governments used taxes to raise operating funds for thousands of years.

   i. Almost any commodity was taxed: land, animals, goods, and imports.

   ii. Taxes reduced the economic power of those being taxed.

   iii. "Tax farming" was used by many governments.

      ➤ Tax farming used local tax collectors to extract money from individuals.

      ➤ The Safavids and Ottomans were two examples of governments who practiced tax farming.

   iv. Some governments, like the Mughal, recognized local elites, called zamindars, as rent collectors of farmers. In exchange for this right to collect rent, the Mughal required their part.

   v. Imported goods ("tariffs") were taxed by almost every government.

2. Inca leaders required farmers to bring their produce to central locations, where government administrators redistributed crops and animals to the rest of the people, especially those in favor.

 ## III. EMPIRES: BELIEF SYSTEMS

Though there were major changes in Christianity and Islam between 1450 and 1750, their basic beliefs remained intact.

A. THE PROTESTANT REFORMATION SPLIT CHRISTIANITY IN WESTERN AND CENTRAL EUROPE

1. In 16th century Central Europe, a reform movement that protested abuses by the Roman Catholic church hierarchy swept across the continent.

i. The Protestant Reformation created a major shake-up of Catholic authority, especially in Northern Europe.

ii. Large European states like Britain and Sweden, and smaller ones within the Holy Roman Empire adopted Protestantism as their official religion.

2. The Roman Catholic church responded with reforms of its own, and maintained its dominance in Southern Europe, and most of Western Europe, and Poland.

i. In Spain especially, spreading the Catholic faith was a major factor in sending voyages to the New World. Missionaries, including Jesuits, were part of these expeditions.

ii. In Islam, an old division intensified—

> ➤ The Ottoman and Safavid empires, although Islamic, were political rivals.

> ➤ Ottomans were mainly of the Sunni branch of Islam and the Safavids were mostly Shi'a. These religious differences intensified their political rivalries, leading to religious/political wars over the Mesopotamian region.

B. IN SOUTH ASIA, A BLENDED FAITH DEVELOPED

1. Sikhism began in the Mughal Empire in this era.

2. Most historians believe Sikhism was a blending of Hindu and Muslim beliefs, through a process called "syncretism." (Another example of a syncretic belief system is Native Americans blending their traditional beliefs with Christianity.)

IV. COMPARISONS OF LAND-BASED EMPIRES

A. This chapter discussed ways states tried to gain and maintain power. To help you remember these comparisons, make Venn diagrams using information about land-based empires.

B. What methods of administration were similar and different? Use specific examples of states and empires.

UNIT 4

Transoceanic Interconnections

c. 1450 to c. 1750

Your studies have reached the point where we can talk about true global history! In the era c. 1450–c. 1750, the Americas, Australia, and the Pacific Islands joined Afro-Eurasia in networks of exchange. The encounters between the peoples of Europe and the Americas had profound social, political, economic, demographic, and environmental effects on both sides of the Atlantic, and then the world.

I. TECHNOLOGICAL INNOVATIONS

Advances in ship design and navigation reached Europe via trade routes from East Asia through the Islamic world of Eurasia. China and India were very advanced compared to Europe at the beginning of this period. These changes benefitted European ship builders, sailors, and scientists.

A. Benefits to Europe from trade with Asia by the end of the previous era included not only spices and other commodities, but also technology. The compass, more accurate maps, the astrolabe (used to determine latitude), and improved rudders and sails—all transferred from Asia—contributed to Europe's ability to make long-distance sailing expeditions.

1. Portuguese shipbuilders introduced the caravel, based on Islamic designs, to explore Africa's Atlantic coast in the 15th century.

2. The introduction of the lateen sail (shaped like a triangle) around 1500 made ships more maneuverable, allowing them to tack, or sail, against the wind and thus extend their voyages into the Indian Ocean and the Atlantic Ocean from the Mediterranean Sea.

B. A "Scientific Revolution" transformed European approaches to science—from haphazard methods to more logical experimentation, concepts picked up from indirect contact with Muslim and Chinese scholars. The telescope, microscope, barometer and new forms of math, such as calculus, are just a few innovations.

II. EXPLORATION: CAUSES AND EVENTS

A. NEW WESTERN EUROPEAN STATES SPONSORED TRANSOCEANIC VOYAGES

1. At the beginning of this era, motivated by "competition" from the Muslim faith in the Mediterranean world, Western European Christians—especially those of Portugal and Spain, who had recently completed a "reconquista" (reconquering) of the Iberian Peninsula from Muslim control—sought to spread their gospel to new areas, particularly South and East Asia, where conversion had thus far been limited. Expeditions almost always included missionaries.

2. The Protestant Reformation caused a renewed missionary vigor among the Catholic monarchs in Western Europe, who did not want their faith to "lose ground" to new and rapidly growing religions.

3. Trade was also a major motivator for European exploration. You've already learned about how the flow of silk, technology, and spices westward from Asia increased wealth and triggered a desire to by-pass the long chain of middlemen that separated European consumers from the riches of the East.

4. The new kings and kingdoms in Spain, Portugal, France, and Britain wanted to display their power by funding explorations.

5. Why Western Europe and not Eastern Europe? Like the nations in Western Europe, Russia also had access to the new shipping technology and sent ships north into the Arctic Ocean seeking a route to East Asia. Icy conditions, however, made that passage impossible. At the same time, Russia was expanding its land empire across Siberia and did not enter the Pacific until the 17th century. Other nations in Central and Eastern Europe had limited access to the sea and/or were not yet organized to mount such expeditions.

B. PORTUGAL LED THE WAY TO NEW LANDS, FOLLOWED BY SPAIN, ENGLAND, FRANCE, AND THE DUTCH

1. Why were Portugal and Spain the first European nations to venture south (Portugal) and west (Spain) into the Atlantic? Geography was a big reason. Both countries "stick out" into the Atlantic more than other European nations. Portugal's proximity to Africa made it a logical target of early coastal exploration. In addition, the newly united nation-state of Spain had just completed a centuries-long campaign to restore the Iberian Peninsula to Christian control. Thus, Spain's leaders had much patriotic energy and were willing to spend money to expand their economic, religious, and political influence beyond their borders.

2. Portugal's Prince Henry the Navigator sent many ships down the western coast of Africa looking for a route to the Indies (islands near India in Southeast Asia), in order to set up direct trade with South Asia. Along the way, they charted the Madeira and the Azores Islands. In 1498, Vasco da Gama succeeded in reaching India and returned to Portugal with spices and other valuable goods. (By the way, one of my all-time favorite lines from a student's essay is, "Flavor and spices were brought back from India by Tabasco da Gama.") The Portuguese finally established their link to the East, but had the Spanish beaten them?

3. Spain sought a different route to the East—they had little choice since the Portuguese staked out Africa's coast, and Italian merchants sailed the Mediterranean for goods.

   i. Spain thought the only land mass on Earth was Afro-Eurasia—so sailing west across the Atlantic would bring a ship straight to the islands near India, the Indies, and maybe even China ("Cathay").

   ii. Columbus convinced the Spanish royals to fund an expedition for God and for gold—in this case, "gold" meant anything of great value, like spices, silk, or gold. Columbus sought glory. Thus we get the famous "Three G's of Exploration"—God, glory, and gold.

   iii. If Columbus were to reach the East and return, he would put Spain ahead of Portugal, which in 1492 was still trying to find India.

4. The Spanish thought Columbus had reached Southeast Asia. Instead, of course, he found a New World. Eventually, his landing place, Cuba, and the surrounding islands, were labeled the "West Indies" and its people were called "Indians"— which shows you how much Spain was aiming for the prize of Southeast Asia's Spice Islands, the real Indies. Over time, however, after Spain began to accumulate great agricultural and mining wealth from the New World, it seemed Columbus's voyages were not the "mistake" that many in Spain thought.

III. THE COLUMBIAN EXCHANGE AND ITS EFFECTS ON THE WORLD

Historians refer to the transfer of animals, plants, diseases, and people that resulted from contacts between Europeans and Amerindians (Native Americans in both North and South America) as the "Columbian Exchange," after the explorer Columbus, who started the process in 1492. Note that this was a two-way exchange, to and from the Americas.

A. ANIMALS AND PLANTS OF THE COLUMBIAN EXCHANGE

1. From Afro-Eurasia to the Americas, Europeans brought horses, pigs, chickens, cows, sugarcane, bananas, wheat, and rice.

2. Effects on the environment were enormous, as you will see.

3. The introduction of horses to the New World changed the cultures of almost every Native American group as the Americas were without large domesticated animals that could be used for transportation and agriculture (unless you want to count the South American llama and alpaca).

4. Sugarcane plantations throughout the Caribbean world helped create rich European kingdoms, and resulted in the importation of slaves from Africa.

5. From the Americas to Afro-Eurasia, Europeans returned with few animals that had a global impact, but among plants, they brought back potatoes, tomatoes, tobacco, American corn (maize), cocoa, as well as chili and other peppers.

   i.   Potato was king in Europe. It stored well on ships and grew in a wide variety of soils and climates.

ii. Maize became a staple in both Africa and China.

iii. Potatoes and maize created unprecedented population growth wherever they were planted. The repercussions of this would be felt for centuries with devastating impacts to traditional societies like China.

B. DISEASES RESULTING FROM THE COLUMBIAN EXCHANGE

1. The greatest effect on the people of the Americas was the introduction of diseases that had not existed in the Western hemisphere before the arrival of the Europeans.

2. Smallpox, in particular, eradicated whole villages of native people, creating a demographic catastrophe that has not been equaled in recorded history.

3. About 90% of the population of the Americas died from these newly-introduced diseases. This de-population created huge open spaces for Europeans to conquer and settle with little resistance.

IV. MARITIME EMPIRES ESTABLISHED

A. EUROPEANS CREATED NEW TRADING POSTS IN AFRICA AND ASIA

1. Portugal was particularly active in creating a global trading-post empire.

   i. On Africa's north coast, it captured the port of Ceuta, which became a jumping-off point for continued port-grabbing on Africa's Atlantic coast. From there, they sailed south and negotiated trade deals with West African kingdoms, like Songhai, usually with military threats.

   ii. Portugal colonized South Africa and continued east into the Indian Ocean, taking over Swahili Coast ports.

   iii. Portugal then conquered Hormuz on the Persian Gulf, Goa on the southwest coast of India, and Malacca in Southeast Asia, leading some to call the Indian Ocean a "Portuguese lake."

2. The Netherlands followed and seized many holdings from Portugal, notably South Africa and what is Indonesia today. Vast European holdings in Africa and Asia became known as "trading post empires."

3. Despite the introduction of Europeans to the Indian Ocean network, trade continued largely as before. Swahili Arabs on the East African coast, Gujaratis merchants on the West Indian coast, and Javanese merchants in Southeast Asia (just to name a few) remained dominant in that region.

4. The main difference between European holdings in Africa and Asia and the Americas is that whole continents were conquered in the Americas, but trading outposts were the norm in Africa and Asia.

5. African and Asian opposition was stronger than in the Americas.

   i. The widespread diseases that brought substantial population loss to the Native American population squelched any chance for significant resistance.

   ii. In Japan, the Tokugawa Shogunate restricted European trading ships to just one a year through one designated point on an island in Nagasaki Bay.

   iii. In China, the Ming Dynasty, who at first in the 16th century sought to restrict foreign trade, were content to send silk and porcelain to Europe in exchange for *lots* of silver from colonies in the Americas. Spanish silver from the Americas was brought to the new Spanish colony of the Philippines for transfer to Chinese markets. In this era, China was the destination for most of the world's silver. This is sometimes known as the global silver drain. The effects of this transfer of wealth from the New World via Spain to China would change each society, causing Spain to suffer bouts of inflation that would later cripple their economic development. China also underwent social changes as the merchant class rose in power at the expense of the state, a new phenomenon in the Confucian world.

   iv. Portugal managed to gain only one port off the coast of China—Macao.

B. EUROPEAN STATES ESTABLISHED NEW MARITIME EMPIRES

1. The Atlantic World is described by the interaction between the four continents on both sides of the Atlantic: North America, South America, Europe, and Africa. Latin America is, of course, also part of the Atlantic World. Britain, France and, to a lesser extent, The Netherlands (Holland/The Dutch) followed Spain and Portugal in establishing colonies in the New World. All held islands in the Caribbean with sugar plantations and competed with each other in that global market.

2. The British, French, and Dutch colonies along the Atlantic coast of North America (i.e., the 13 colonies) were an afterthought. They were not a big economic factor compared to the wealth of metals and sugar coming out of Latin America.

   i. The biggest economic contribution from the colonies of *upper* North America—remember, the Caribbean and Mexico are considered part of North America as well—was a species of fish. Cod was enormously popular among people on both sides of the Atlantic. Its presence off the coast of Massachusetts, near Cape Cod, made European monarchs give colonization there a try.

3. Initially, Spanish explorers were not settlers and few women made the early voyages. Mixed-race children were born out of relationships between Spaniards and Native women. Slowly, European women made the dangerous trip to the New World and European-only families began to form. Thus, a new social hierarchy was created, with skin color being the determining factor in status.

4. The American empires that didn't benefit from the growth of European-based maritime empires were the Aztec (Mexica) in central Mexico and the Inca in northern South America. They collapsed from a combination of internal political conflicts, the destruction of their population from disease, and pressure from Spanish conquistadors.

C. SHORTAGE OF LABOR AND SLAVERY IN THE NEW WORLD

1. The high mortality rates of natives on sugarcane plantations resulted in a severe shortage of labor.

   i. Portugal was first among the European nations to enslave Africans along Africa's Atlantic coast, and haul them to their sugarcane plantations in Brazil.

   ii. Spain followed suit, transporting Africans bought along the "Slave Coast" in packed ships across the Atlantic (the Middle Passage) to Caribbean sugar plantations.

   iii. This form of slavery that involves buying humans was called chattel slavery.

 2. West African kingdoms continued to trade slaves within Africa and to Arab and Indian Ocean locales.

   i. Exporting slaves into the Mediterranean and Indian Ocean areas by Muslim Arabs intensified because of the need for labor.

   ii. The Asante and the Kingdom of the Kongo gained power to expand their territory by trading goods such as guns, salt, and animal skins for slaves.

 3. Under the *encomienda* system, Spanish colonists used Amerindians who survived the disease pandemics for their labor needs. The Spanish crown granted conquistadors and settlers large tracts of land called *haciendas*, and on them, native laborers worked the land, farming and/or raising cattle or, in the case of Peru working in the world's largest silver mine at Potosi.

 4. The Incan *mit'a* system that required its populations to perform public works service was adapted by the Spanish to become a system of forced labor. Complaints of abuse by church and some government officials in Latin America led the crown in Spain to end these systems by the early 18th century.

 5. Indentured servants were enlisted when slaves were unavailable, such as in the British colonies of Virginia and Maryland.

   i. In the British colonies, particularly Virginia and Maryland, an indentured servant of British origin was a "temporary slave" for about seven years. At the end of servitude, an indentured servant was free of obligations to his or her master.

   ii. Thousands migrated to the British colonies as indentured servants and, if they survived, established their own destinies in the New World.

Changes in labor systems during this era is a frequent subject of test items on the AP® World History: Modern exam.

D. THE PLANTATION ECONOMY'S GROWTH MEANT CHANGE: DEMOGRAPHIC, SOCIAL, AND CULTURAL

1. In their zeal to spread the holy word, Catholic missionaries in the Portuguese and Spanish territories held mass baptisms with little religious instruction. Thus, the traditions of the original faiths of the natives continued with Christian beliefs woven in.

2. Africans were forcibly taken to the Americas as slaves, initially to sugarcane plantations in Brazil and the Caribbean. The massive loss of people out of Africa—mostly men—damaged African demography. With so many men gone, population declined, as did social stability.

3. Some Europeans (like those from the Spanish-held Canary Islands) were also re-settled to the Americas against their will as colonists and/or indentured servants.

4. Latin American society was a blend of European, African, and Native American cultures. Food, faith, family structure, and racial identities were affected by the contacts between these groups over many centuries. This blending and the social structures that emerged in Latin America is often referred to as the *sociedad de las castas*. This system attempted to create hierarchical distinctions between people in the New World based upon the extent of native or African ancestry. This will be discussed in more detail later in this chapter.

V. MARITIME EMPIRES MAINTAINED AND DEVELOPED

A. MERCANTILISM EXPANDED MARITIME EMPIRES

1. *Mercantilism* is defined as a government policy to ensure exports exceed imports.

   i. European monarchs extracted raw materials from the colonies, and then manufactured products from those materials to sell globally. The reason was to have a positive balance of trade.

   ii. Governments imposed taxes—tariffs—on imported products from rival nations.

2. The first global trade network was established.

   i. Silver from the Americas was traded for Asian spices, silk, porcelain, and other commodities Europeans desired. Japan joined this network because it, too, had silver mines. China and India were buyers of most of the silver.

   ii. The *triangle trade* system of the Atlantic World is familiar to most AP® World History: Modern students.

> Sugar, rum (which comes from fermented sugarcane), and cod were shipped from the New World to Europe. They were traded for silver or commercial products, which were then shipped to Africa and exchanged for slaves.

> Slaves were then sent to the New World.

   iii. European governments also went into business with private companies that traded globally.

> With government cooperation, private companies made and enforced their own laws, approved ship schedules and cargoes, and negotiated commerce agreements with rulers globally.

> The British East India Company, the Muscovy Company (a group of English merchants who traded with Russia), and the Dutch East India Company (abbreviated as the "VOC"*) are famous examples of what were called joint-stock companies in which investors pooled their finances to fund the establishment of colonies they hoped would be profitable. The Virginia Colony at Jamestown was founded by a joint-stock company.

B. ECONOMICS IN AFRICA AND ASIA

1. The era c. 1450—c. 1750 involved more than commerce across the Atlantic Ocean.

---

* "VOC" abbreviates the Dutch: Vereenigde Oostindische Compagnie

2. In the Indian Ocean region, trade flourished among the traditional participants such as the Swahili Arabs, Omanis, and Gujaritis from East Africa, South Asia, Southeast Asia, and East Asia.

3. European merchants had to cooperate with local rulers of port cities because they could not dominate this long-standing trade culture on their own. That was one reason Atlantic World trade surpassed that of the Indian Ocean network by the middle of this era.

4. Globally, most people remained farmers.

    i. Many were subsistence farmers, that is, growing enough for their family with a little left over to sell.

    ii. Others harvested a single crop for a landowner for export—the beginnings of commercial farming.

    iii. Changes involved the crop being grown because of the influx of new foods from the Americas—corn in China, for example.

5. In the late 1500s in West Africa, the sultan of Morocco defeated neighboring Songhai forces to take control of its Trans-Sahara trade routes, and the Songhai Empire collapsed.

C. CHANGES IN ASIAN LABOR SYSTEMS

1. The inclusion of the New World into the global systems of exchange expanded the world economy.

2. This expanded economy impacted the operation of labor systems around the world.

    i. As a result of increased requirements for goods to trade on the new global market, Russia expanded into Siberia and began to export valuable furs, especially into the newly-rich European market. Peasants were involved in the trapping and processing of the furs. Peasants also farmed large tracts of land owned by Russia's elite class. Peru's potato became a staple in Russia's diet.

    ii. In India, hand-woven cotton products were churned out by crafters for export.

    iii. Chinese peasants were involved in silk production.

D. ALONG WITH TRADE, RELIGIONS SPREAD TO NEW LANDS

1. The surest way to become a global religion is to adapt to local customs. This process of merging various beliefs is called *syncretism*.

   i. Christianity, in its Catholic form, syncretized in Latin America. With official sponsorship from both the Church and European rulers, missionaries in Latin America succeeded, but the religion that emerged, after encounters with traditional beliefs, was different. In Mexico, for example, many Christian saints took on the same duties as the pre-colonial gods they replaced. As had been done before Christianity arrived, offerings were made and votive candles lit in prayer asking for divine intercession. In the Caribbean, a mix of indigenous African religions and Christianity merged to produce Vodun, or voodoo.

   ii. Islam spread as it had in the earlier era into sub-Saharan regions, East and Southeast Asia, including parts of the Philippines.

   iii. Buddhism continued to spread across Southeast Asia and into parts of Central Asia.

   iv. Hinduism remained the core religion of India.

2. People yet to be contacted by Buddhists, Christians, or Muslims continued to practice their indigenous faiths.

VI. INTERNAL AND EXTERNAL CHALLENGES TO LAND AND MARITIME EMPIRES, c. 1450–c. 1750

Indigenous people often rejected the influences of outsiders, and slaves resisted the system imposed on them.

A. Examples of local resistance include Pueblo revolts against Spanish rule in present-day New Mexico and Cossack revolts against the Russian empire, both in the 17th century. In the North American British colonies, Native American leader Metacom ("King Philip") waged war against colonials in New England.

B. Examples of slave resistance in the Americas range from sabotaging tools, slowing labor, and running away to form separate colonies away from plantations. These "Maroon societies" were distributed all over the Caribbean and Central America. The largest was in Brazil, had a king, and lasted almost 100 years. It was finally conquered by Portuguese forces at the end of the 17th century.

VII. CHANGING SOCIAL HIERARCHIES

As expected, contacts between the New and Old Worlds had profound effects that are still felt today. In this era, many societies changed.

A. POLITICAL ELITES

1. European royalty marked friends and relatives with titles of nobility, such as "lord" and "marquis." These aristocrats claimed privileges that the "lesser" classes only dreamed they could have. With their high status, many nobles also considered themselves to be stewards of the poor and patrons of the arts.

2. The new ruling class in Latin America was the Creole elites. Early settlers in the New World who were born in Spain or Portugal were called the *Peninsulares*, after the Iberian Peninsula. They were at the top of Latin American society and government. Below that on the societal pyramid were the Creoles, i.e., Europeans born in the New World. Over time, as the numbers of Peninsulares faded and the numbers of Creoles increased, the distinction faded as well.

3. Below the elites in Latin America were various mixed-race peoples, called *Mestizos*. Essentially, the more European "blood" a person had (or, conveniently, the whiter the skin), the higher they stood on the social ladder. The more Amerindian or African people appeared, the lower they were on the social ladder. This was known as the *sociedad de las castas* or *Casta* system.

4. In the North American British and French colonies, there was much less mixing of races. The Europeans established themselves at the top of colonial society, but there was a pecking order among the whites, with European indentured servants below the ruling elites, but above Indians and African slaves.

B. ECONOMIC ELITES

1. In Europe and the Americas, new economic elites arose from the merchant class. Entrepreneurs successful in global trade were rewarded with financial success and social status.

2. In China, merchants had low social status, but enjoyed the benefits of wealth.

3. In Asia, outside of China, wealthy merchants were members of the social elite in every major port city in the Indian Ocean network, Korea, and Japan.

C. STATE SUPPRESSION

1. Typically, governments set policies to limit the rights of various groups.

   i. In the Americas, slaves had no meaningful rights and few privileges.

   ii. In Europe, Jews were so persecuted that many fled and settled elsewhere, particularly in the Ottoman Empire.

   iii. In China, the Manchus defeated the Ming and became the new elite ruling class in the Qing Dynasty. The majority Han people were barred from settling on Manchu land and were required to wear their hair in a "queue" as a sign of submission to the Manchu.

UNIT 5

Revolutions

c. 1750 to c. 1900

There were many types of revolutions in the era c. 1750–c. 1900: political, intellectual, and industrial, for starters. Ideas from European-based Enlightenment philosophies sparked revolutionary ideas founded on concepts of liberty and equality that remain vital today.

I. NEW VIEWS ON NATURE AND HUMAN RELATIONSHIPS

The Enlightenment was an era of new ideas in Western thought about approaches to religion, art, government, science, and philosophy. The movement peaked in the 18th century in Europe, but because its culture spread globally during the Age of Imperialism (see Chapter 9), Enlightenment ideas did too.

A. ENLIGHTENMENT

Concepts from the Scientific Revolution (see Chapter 7) sparked European intellectuals to think that the human condition could be explained and improved if scientifically-based rational thought governed everyday life. Applied to politics, such ideals were labelled "classical liberalism." For example:

1. **Individual equality.** Enlightenment thinkers (*philosophes*, French for "philosophers"), such as the French writers Voltaire and Rousseau, advocated that all men were created equal— that no person deserved extra privileges over others just for being born. A king was not automatically "better" than a commoner. The U.S. Declaration of Independence reflects this belief.

2. **Individual liberty.** This Enlightenment ideal says people should be free to make their own personal and economic decisions in life. Freedom of speech and religion were "natural rights"

given by God, not man. Slavery should be abolished. Women should be treated as political equals to men. Famous European writers promoting women's rights were Mary Wollstonecraft (*A Vindication of the Rights of Women*) and Olympe de Gouges (*Declaration of the Rights of Woman and the Female Citizen*).

3. **Limited governments.** Enlightenment thinkers Locke and Rousseau wrote that governments and the people had a "social contract" between them. If the leader of the government failed to serve the people well, the people had a right to revolt. Favored forms of government among Enlightenment thinkers included a constitution, freedom of thought, and divided powers between a king and a legislature. Other philosophes favored these ideas, but without a king. They sought a government led by a leader elected by popular vote.

B. **NATIONALISM**

1. Nationalism arose from Enlightenment thought about personal liberties and choices. It inspired many to call for the creation of new nations out of large empires.

2. *Nationalism* is defined as a sense of strong identity with others who share a common history, customs, religion, and/or language. This concept was a major factor in the independence movements in Latin America and Europe in the 19th century, and colonies worldwide in the 20th century.

 II. **NATIONALISM AND REVOLUTIONS FROM 1750 TO 1900: POLITICS IN THE ATLANTIC WORLD**

A. **AMERICAN REVOLUTION**

1. The first place these ideas about revolution were tried on a large scale was in the British colonies in America.

2. The Declaration of Independence spelled out Enlightenment ideas of "life, liberty and the pursuit of happiness." In the context of World History, the effects of the American Revolution were enormous.

3. The notion that a group of colonies could overthrow a European power and establish—on purpose, no less—a

representative government based on Enlightenment principles, inspired revolutions around the world into the 21st century.

B. FRENCH REVOLUTION AND AFTERMATH

1. In 1789, the French revolted against their king, Louis XVI, but unlike the American Revolution, the struggle was not with a colony but in the home country. In the spirit of Enlightenment ideas, the slogan of the French Revolution was, "Liberty, Equality, Fraternity (brotherhood)." The French Revolution expressed its roots in the Enlightenment in the civil rights document, "Declaration of the Rights of Man and the Citizen."

2. After failing to create a limited constitutional monarchy similar to Britain's, French leaders established a republic. But they insisted on radically reshaping political and cultural traditions to fit their goals.

3. The French Republic was overthrown by Napoleon Bonaparte, a military dictator who restored order. Claiming to be a "child of the Enlightenment," he did enact reforms, such as equality, before the law. But he was no supporter of republican government. After Napoleon's defeat by a coalition of other European nations, European boundaries were reorganized which added new nations such as a new version of the Netherlands.

C. HAITI AND LATIN AMERICA

1. Haiti

   i. The French Revolution's first "child" was delivered in the early 19th century in its colony of Haiti, then known as Saint-Domingue. The vast majority of the residents were slaves. Led by Toussaint L'Ouverture, they revolted against their white French masters. An army sent by Napoleon to quell the rebellion was defeated.

   ii. The result of this first successful slave revolt was the establishment of the second republic in the New World, after the U.S.

   iii. In its revolution, Haiti's rich plantation economy of large exportable crops of sugar and coffee was destroyed and replaced by small farms that exported very little.

Test Tip

Be sure to know the similarities and differences between the Haitian and French revolutions, and the communist revolution in Russia.

2. Latin America

i. By 1830, the successful Haitian revolution inspired the rest of Latin America's colonies to rise against Spanish and Portuguese rule. Led by upper class "Creole elites"— most famously Simón Bolívar—one by one the colonies gained independence through military victories against the colonizers, hastening the decline of Spain as a world power. Bolívar wrote a Latin American "Declaration of Independence" known as "The Jamaica Letter."

ii. Unlike the U.S., which had a sizable educated middle class, in Latin America there was an enormous social and economic chasm between the few elite and the many poor. Similar to the U.S. experience, the elite remained in power after the revolutions. Establishing stable governments proved difficult in the new Latin American nations, including Mexico and Brazil, as was a lack of significant social and economic change for the non-elites.

iii. Although women's rights were frequently discussed by the European philosophes, in Latin America and elsewhere, they were largely set aside until the 20th century.

D. "EUROPE IN FLAMES"

1. The nationalist revolutions in Latin America expelled the colonial powers. These successes inspired Europeans to use nationalism to replace governments thought to be "outside oppressors." Greece broke away from the Ottoman Empire (1820). But in the vast Austrian empire, Poles, Italians, and Slavs, failed to break away and form their own nations in the early 19th century. In 1848, so many nations experienced violence—in some cases civil war—that the phrase "Europe in flames" became popular. In the 1860s and 1870s, two new nations emerged, both forged with strong nationalist fervor: Italy and Germany.

2. In 1830 and 1848, dissatisfied French rebels overthrew their governments. In the second of these revolutions, France established another short-lived republic.

3. In Russia in the 1820s, a military coup promising a constitutional monarchy failed miserably, but inspired future revolutionaries there.

III. THE INDUSTRIAL REVOLUTION BEGINS

A. HISTORIC IMPACT

1. In the era c. 1750–c. 1900, the greatest revolution since the Neolithic era (c. 8000 BCE) occurred: the Industrial Revolution. It fundamentally changed the human experience and continues to affect the world today. Although some people in the early 21st century have not experienced industrialization directly, only a miniscule number can be said to be unaffected by it.

2. The Industrial Revolution changed governments, family life, global and local economies, food production, migration, war, art and literature, the environment, transportation, communication, population growth, and rural and urban areas. It led to the Age of Imperialism, political revolutions, communism, World War I, women's rights, multinational corporations, and the "traditional" Western family.

B. CAUSES OF THE INDUSTRIAL REVOLUTION

Why did the Industrial Revolution begin in Western Europe, and why specifically in Britain? Several factors contributed.

1. Government policies—As noted in previous chapters, Western Europe built political and economic empires in the New World. The flow of silver and gold from the New World into Europe's treasuries made their societies the richest in the world. European governments—especially Britain—invested part of this income in the form of monetary prizes to individuals who invented more efficient ways to transport goods, grow crops, defeat enemies—anything that might significantly contribute to growing the nation's slice of the global mercantilist pie. (See Chapter 7.)

2. Geography—A major environmental cause was selecting the right type of natural resources to create the inventions.

   i. Britain had coal, timber, and iron, rich soil, fast-moving rivers to turn waterwheels that powered machines, and many natural harbors to import raw materials from faraway colonies. Products manufactured from those raw materials were exported back to millions of colonial consumers and other markets around the globe.

   ii. Belgium, Germany, and France had similar favorable geographic conditions and were quick to follow Britain's lead in developing industry.

3. Economic and Social Mobility

   i. In Britain, and to a lesser degree in the rest of Western Europe, citizens could move up the economic and social ladder by developing a money-making invention. This incentive spurred Britain to become "a nation of tinkerers," as one observer put it. Banks loaned money to entrepreneurs in whom they had faith.

   ii. European governments offered prizes for inventions that they considered helpful to their global economic and political goals. These conditions did not exist outside Europe at the beginning of this era.

4. Workforce

   i. Britain had many workers skilled in operating metal tools. Those skills were necessary for the creation of the machines that would be used to develop its industry.

   ii. Many British agricultural workers were forced off farmland by a government-approved policy called the Enclosure Movement. The landless peasants migrated to cities, forming a large potential workforce for factories.

C. BEGINNINGS OF THE INDUSTRIAL REVOLUTION

1. Mechanization of Textile Production

   i. British inventors developed machines that mass-produced cloth and thread. These muscle-powered wood-and-iron machines cranked out cloth faster and cheaper than hand-made materials.

  ii. Bigger and quicker machines were developed and amassed into large buildings called factories. Waterwheels rotating in fast-moving streams provided power for the machines.

2. Uses of steam engine

  i. By the 1760s, British inventors had developed the steam engine—one of the most revolutionary inventions of all time—and made water power obsolete. No longer did factories have to be anchored next to a stream; they could be located anywhere.

  ii. Connecting cloth- and thread-making machines to steam engines increased production many times beyond what humans could do. Mass production of goods made machine-made clothing affordable to just about all Europeans.

3. More inventions.

  i. The cotton gin removed seeds from cotton to prepare it for thread and cloth manufacturing. It operated many times faster than any human and when hooked to a steam engine, even faster.

  ii. Two early 19th-century inventions involving the steam engine drastically altered transportation. In the U.S., the first steamboat made sail power obsolete. In Britain, the steam-powered locomotives on railroads marked the beginning of the end of the age of the horse in modern societies.

  iii. The steamboat created more reliable, faster, and cheaper transoceanic travel. This caused a huge increase in the numbers of people migrating from one region to another, most significantly from Europe to the Americas.

IV. THE SPREAD OF INDUSTRIALIZATION

The Industrial Revolution spread from Britain to the U.S., then to Japan, Russia, Latin America, and India.

A. UNITED STATES

1. Thanks to the cotton gin, single-crop plantations in the South became highly profitable.

2. British-style factories that turned American cotton into textiles popped up in the Northeast. The South produced so much cotton that the surplus was sold to British factories. Slavery was abolished after the U.S. Civil War giving the industrial North an even bigger economic boost over the South.

3. Railroads sprang up, first in the Northeast, and soon connected to farming areas in the Midwest and South, speeding delivery of crops and farm animals to processing factories in Chicago and other Northern cities.

4. By 1900, the U.S. was the world's biggest steel producer. U.S. Steel Corporation became the first billion-dollar corporation.

B. LATIN AMERICA

1. Europeans invested heavily to jump-start industrialization in Latin America. Great expectations followed and some railroad routes were built, but overall, like Russia, Latin America remained largely an exporter of crops grown by peasant labor. Among their products were coffee, bananas, wheat, beef, and sugar. Industrialized nations sought Mexican copper.

C. INDIA

1. Britain established its rule (raj) over India early in the era c. 1750–c.1900.

2. India was a leading grower of cotton, and Britain eagerly imported the processed fabric for its textile mills. Under British authority, Indian textile factories began to produce machine-made cotton thread and cloth, and the production of hand-made textiles began to decline.

3. India's age of rapid industrial growth, however, languished until the late 20th century.

D. INDUSTRIALIZATION IN OTHER REGIONS

1. The Ottoman Empire was slow in developing modern industries. Its leaders failed to recognize the extent to which industrialization was increasing the West's political, economic, and military power. Unlike the Japanese, the Ottoman leadership was divided over following Western Europe's industrial model.

2. Africa remained a provider of natural resources to the world's industrial giants.

   i. The greatest export in terms of value were diamonds and gold from South Africa.

   ii. In the Age of Imperialism (see Chapter 9), Europe's governments and businesses kept its African colonies dependent on them.

3. China rejected Western ideas in this era and remained largely out of the production end of the Industrial Revolution. Some foreign investment provided for railroads and steamships, but overall, the Middle Kingdom stuck with human labor to produce crops and hand-made items for export.

Questions comparing industrialization in the West and other regions <u>will</u> appear on the exam.

V. TECHNOLOGY OF THE INDUSTRIAL AGE

A. FOSSIL FUELS FED INDUSTRY

1. Coal was the initial fuel for the early steam engines, but as the 19th century progressed, petroleum was increasingly used, especially after the development of the internal combustion (diesel and later, gasoline) engine. Both provided vastly greater amounts of energy than any previous form of power.

B. STEEL BECOMES THE "KING OF METALS"

1. Advancements in steel processing led to mass production of this alloy that was stronger, lighter, and more flexible than iron. Factories were built in regions near iron and coal mines, materials vital to steel production. Western Europe again led the way, soon followed by the U.S., Japan, and Russia. Steel became *the* metal of the Industrial Age.

C. THE "SECOND INDUSTRIAL REVOLUTION"

1. The pace of industrialization quickened and so did the number of inventions in the second half of the 19th century. This "Second Industrial Revolution" was different from the first. Instead of focusing on textile production and steam power, the Second Industrial Revolution ran on the internal combustion (gasoline or diesel) system. Also, more inventions were related to electrical systems, scientific discoveries, and medicine. Many had applications for the mechanization of warfare.

2. Communications. The first major development was the American invention of the telegraph in the 1840s. By the late 1850s, a telegraph cable was extended under the Atlantic, linking the British Isles to Canada and the U.S. By the 1870s, communication across the Pacific was achieved, and by 1902, the entire global British empire was connected by telegraph.

    i. In 1876, the telephone was invented in the U.S. Its popularity was greater than the telegraph because the user needed no special training, making it a consumer product.

    ii. The radio (or "wireless telegraph") was being developed near the end of this era.

3. Transportation. After the steamboat and steam train, the next major step in transportation was the electric trolley car and the subterranean transportation system, or subway.

    i. Both the trolley and the subway were mass-transit systems, first used in large cities like London, Paris, and New York.

    ii. The automobile was invented in Germany in the 1880s. In this era, it was mostly an experimental machine and an object of curiosity.

    iii. Improved transportation such as ocean-crossing steamboats led to massive migrations, especially from Europe to the Americas in the late 19th and early 20th centuries.

VI. INDUSTRIALIZATION: GOVERNMENT'S ROLE

Most participants in the Industrial Revolution had governments that guided its development. The federal government's power rose dramatically after the American Civil War, and it adopted a strong pro-industry attitude. The U.S. courts favored business development over workers' rights. In 1869, the U.S. completed the east-to-west Transcontinental Railroad, the world's longest at the time.

A. MEIJI JAPAN

1. Using a show of industrial force, the American government sent navy ships to force open the trade door with Japan in the 1850s. The Japanese government responded not by resisting, like China, but by transforming its government, society, and industry.

2. The Tokugawa Shogunate was replaced by the Meiji Restoration, with a Western-style constitutional monarchy. The Japanese built railroads, modernized their military, and constructed factories that specialized in silk textiles.

3. One significant difference between Japanese and Western industrialization was that the Japanese government had close ties to factory corporations. The government built factories, then sold them to investors, but stayed actively involved in their finances and business decisions.

B. RUSSIA

1. Unlike Japan and the "West," Russia's industrial progress was limited. The government's primary focus was on supporting the elite owners of large agricultural estates. Serfdom was still in place until the mid-19th century. The government freed the serfs, but unlike the U.S. and Japan, Russia was slow to shift to industrialization.

2. Late in this era, the Russian government sought foreign investment in its industrial program. Russia became a top producer of steel, and built the Trans-Siberian Railway, surpassing the U.S. in boasting the world's longest railroad. Despite these accomplishments, Russia's economy remained largely mired in the 15th century. Peasant laborers grew mostly wheat and potatoes for export from the large estates still owned by friends of the czar.

C. EGYPT

1. Under the leadership of Muhammad Ali, the Egyptian government attempted to jump start the Industrial Revolution by building railroads, dams, and cotton factories.

2. Egypt also agreed to let the French construct the Suez Canal connecting the Red Sea to the Mediterranean Sea, using human labor and steam shovels.

 VII. ECONOMIC DEVELOPMENTS IN THE INDUSTRIAL AGE

In the late 1700s, Scottish economist Adam Smith insisted that governments end their mercantilist policies, engage in free trade (drop tariffs on imports from other countries) and stay out of the way of the "natural" cycles of the economy of boom and bust. This economic theory is "laissez-faire" capitalism, and caught on big-time in Western Europe in the 19th century.

A. Transnational corporations grew in number. With the ever-expanding global market for machine-made goods came businesses that operated on a global scale. Insurance companies, such as the British-based Lloyd's of London, wrote policies around the world. HSBC is a multinational banking corporation, also based in Britain. U.S.-based United Fruit Corporation operated banana plantations throughout Central America, with its produce shipped to the U.S. and Europe.

B. Governments took legal steps to protect transnational businesses, such as limiting how much financial liability a corporation could face if sued by a consumer. These are called limited-liability corporations.

C. The exchange of goods and money among the industrialized economies grew so fast that they established a "gold standard" for world currencies. An agreed-upon international price of gold became the measure by which nations determined the relative value of their money systems. Stock markets in major financial centers like London and New York encouraged investments of capital from the middle and wealthy classes.

The growth of transnational corporations is a frequent topic on the AP® World History: Modern exam.

VIII. REACTIONS TO THE INDUSTRIAL ECONOMY

A. WESTERN EUROPE AND THE U.S.

1. The Industrial Revolution resulted in more and larger cities. Seeking a steady income, people practically fled farm life and moved to cities to work in industrial jobs. With the boom in urban population came overcrowded living conditions, high levels of pollution, higher crime rates, and a poor and increasingly discontent working class. Pressures from these conditions led to proposals for sweeping changes in government policies, particularly in Europe and the U.S.

2. Pressures in cities and factories

   i. Overcrowded cities created many problems: a shortage of decent housing, disease, and unemployment to name a few.

   ii. The lower classes suffered the most and discontent spilled into the streets of many major European cities. Poor working conditions in factories, including hazardous machinery, long hours, and low pay led to anger and resentment among the laboring classes.

   iii. Government leaders were often slow to respond to the calls for reform because they were either overwhelmed by or did not care about the numerous problems facing societies in the early years of the Industrial Revolution.

   iv. By the mid-19th century, however, political pressure from the increasingly important middle class stirred governments in Western and Central Europe to begin providing assistance to the urban working classes.

3. Calls for change

   i. From the 1820s through the 1840s, European activists rallied the urban poor to take to the streets. The middle class was urged to use its new voting power to call for political rights for working-class men, increased pay, and safer working conditions in factories.

ii. Only a few men and women lobbied for voting rights for women in the early 19th century.

iii. Labor unions, representing the collective power of many workers began to form. The labor unions were illegal in most Western European nations until later in the 19th century.

4. Karl Marx was considered the most radical activist among those calling for political change. In 1848, commenting on the plight of the working poor in London, Marx's "Communist Manifesto" demanded overthrow of the "haves" ("bourgeoisie") by the "have-nots" ("proletariat"). He envisioned the creation of a classless society where all people were politically, socially, and economically equal. At the time, the few people who read his materials thought these ideas had no chance of success.

5. Those in the new middle class did not take to the streets in support of the urban poor, but they did effect change with their new political rights. For example, they convinced government leaders to provide police services and cleaner drinking water in London, to build public housing in Paris, and to establish unemployment and social security benefits in the new nation of Germany.

B. REACTIONS BEYOND THE WEST

1. The Ottoman Empire's attempts to westernize and compete with Western Europe in the 19th century, consisted of a movement toward a constitutional government—the Tanzimat Reforms—and the purchase of modern weapons from European manufacturers.

i. *Tanzimat* means "reorganization" and that is what the reforms did to the Ottoman government. A written constitution with guaranteed political and social rights, including freedom of religion, a modernized banking system, railroad construction, and reorganization and modernization of the army were some of the major changes.

ii. After 40 years under this first constitution, the Ottoman leader, the Sultan, canceled it and dissolved the legislature in 1876. He realized changes to the constitution called for limitations of his own powers.

iii. Later, another reform movement came from within the military. The "Young Turks" were Western-educated young army officers in the early 20th century who sought revival and extension of the Tanzimat reforms. They succeeded, but after World War I, the 700-year-old empire collapsed and was divided into many nations.

iv. Like the Russians, the Ottoman Empire had limited progress in developing modern industry in this era. The empire's leaders failed to recognize the degree to which the Industrial Revolution was increasing the West's political, economic, and military power. Unlike Japan's leaders at this time, the Ottomans were divided over following Western Europe's industrial model.

2. The African continent remained a provider of natural resources to the world's industrial giants. The greatest export in terms of cost were diamonds and gold from South Africa. In the Age of Imperialism (see Chapter 9), Europe's governments and businesses preferred to keep its African colonies dependent on them.

3. As you have learned, Qing China rejected most things Western in this era and remained largely out of the Industrial Revolution. Some foreign investment provided for railroads and steamships, but overall the Middle Kingdom stayed with human labor to produce crops and hand-made items for export. Western Europe, the U.S., Russia, and Japan took advantage of China's weak government by forcing open exclusive trade regions—"Spheres of Influence"—in China. So Russia traded in one region of China, Britain in another, and France in yet another. At the end of this era, these nations accepted a U.S. proposal for an "Open Door Policy" in China, ending the "Spheres of Influence" and allowing open access to all of its markets.

IX. SOCIETY AND THE INDUSTRIAL AGE

A. CAUSES OF CHANGES IN SOCIETIES

1. In Western countries, the rapid changes that industrialization had on the economy affected everyday life as well. In Britain, the factory system demanded a great deal of labor so men, women, and children moved from farms to cities to work in textile and other kinds of factories. Another factor in the move from farms to cities was the loss of farm jobs due to the increased use of labor-saving devices in agriculture.

B. EFFECTS OF INDUSTRIALIZATION ON SOCIETIES

1. Over time, wages rose so much that working outside the home became primarily a "man's job." As factories became more efficient, less human labor was required, so, for the most part, women and children left factory work. However, in many areas of the West, children continued to work in coal mines and in agricultural labor.

2. As steady wages increased over time, a new social class arose in the industrial West: the middle class. This economic and social group between the rich and the poor had always existed, but in this era, it exploded in size and political power.

3. As fewer children were needed for factory work because of increased efficiency of machinery, Western governments concerned about unsupervised, idle children passed laws requiring school attendance.

4. Middle-class women were expected to marry and stay home to care for their families. These values created what we now call the "traditional family structure." Urban families had fewer children than their rural counterparts. Single women increasingly found employment as teachers, replacing men. As the 20th century approached, women began to replace men in the business environment as secretaries and telephone operators. They were not allowed to vote in most Western societies until after World War I.

> *The AP® World History: Modern exam has been known to ask questions about the effects of industrialization on Japanese society especially on the conditions young women endured who were sent from rural areas by their families to work in silk factories. Unhealthy working conditions and threats from male supervisors were the subject of songs and poems written by "factory girls."*

5. The limited impact of the Industrial Revolution on Latin America meant that continuities in social structures and gender roles remained through this era. In another major social development, millions of Europeans migrated to Latin America seeking new economic opportunities. In an interesting parallel, thousands of Japanese immigrants poured into the west coast of South America, mostly to work as laborers. (See Chapter 9.)

C. ART AND LITERATURE

The Industrial Revolution even affected art and literature. Is there anything it couldn't do?!

1. Looking at the gritty life of overcrowded industrial cities, artists abandoned the optimism of the Romantic school of art of the early 19th century and shifted to Realism, painting dark scenes of city life, exemplified by locomotives belching black smoke.

   i. One new invention was the camera, which artists feared would put them out of business.

   ii. The artistic style called Impressionism was in direct contrast to photography's graphic realism. Artists painted deliberately unfocused scenes of nature—their "impression" of the scene. French artists led the way in this school of art.

2. Writers also responded to the effects of the Industrial Revolution. Charles Dickens wrote stories about life among the struggling urban laboring classes in soot-covered London in the early 19th century in his classics *A Christmas Carol* and *Oliver Twist*.

D. SCIENCE AND MEDICINE

Enormous advances were made in the fields of scientific discoveries and medicine.

1. The modern science of chemistry began in this era. Systematic studies of chemical compounds and the composition of different forms of matter gave scientists insights into how nature works. Toward the end of the era, scientists were developing chemical compounds in the lab; some were powerful fertilizers used to grow bigger crops (and thus more food, leading to more people) than ever before.

2. Advances in medicine included smallpox and rabies vaccinations, sterilization of surgical instruments, the use of anesthetics to "knock out" patients during surgery, and aspirin, to name a few. Governments oversaw programs that provided clean drinking water in cities. These and many other examples led to healthier, longer lives in the industrialized world.

3. Scientific developments and faith crossed swords in Charles Darwin. His investigations of animals of the South Pacific led him to conclude that natural selection, not God, determined the viability of species on Earth. He also theorized that man and apes had similar characteristics, and must therefore have common ancestors. These pronouncements began furious debates about the nature of mankind and its place among fellow humans and animals in the world. His ideas about "survival of the fittest" in the animal kingdoms led some Europeans to transfer the concept to human civilizations. *Social Darwinism*—wherein the superior races must naturally defeat inferior ones—had enormous implications in the Age of Imperialism (see Chapter 9).

X. CONTINUITY AND CHANGE IN THE INDUSTRIAL AGE

This chapter has outlined the enormous changes brought to societies by the Industrial Revolution. However, as always, some things stayed the same. For example, patriarchy in society remained, although women in industrialized countries began to see some political and economic gains. In sub-Saharan Africa and much of Asia, the Industrial Revolution was non-existent. Most people still maintained a religious belief; in Europe and the Americas, Christianity was predominant while from West Africa to Central Asia, Islam remained the primary faith.

Make a chart that tracks similar and different reactions to the Industrial Revolution in Europe, Japan, the Ottoman Empire, and China. Explain those similarities and differences.

Consequences of Industrialization

c. 1750 to c. 1900

I. INTRODUCTION

This chapter focuses on the causes and effects of Imperialism—the movement by many newly industrialized states in the 19th and early 20th centuries to build empires of colonies around the world. In the 21st century, the term "global empire" has a negative connotation, but one hundred years ago, all advanced countries sought an empire. The Western European powers—and to a lesser extent the U.S. and Japan—established empires outside their borders. Western Europe's empires were global, with territories in Africa, Asia, North and South America, Australia and islands in the Pacific, Atlantic, and Indian Oceans.

You remember reading about the first era of European imperialism in the 16th and 17th centuries. Then, the focus was on the Americas. In the late 18th and through the 19th centuries, the nations of Europe restarted the process, but this time Africa and Asia were the primary targets. Ironically, during this age of "new" Imperialism, Spain and Portugal, two of the greatest empires of the previous era, began to decline in global power.

II. RATIONALES FOR IMPERIALISM FROM 1750 TO 1900

A. THE INDUSTRIAL REVOLUTION

1. Using inventions of the Industrial Revolution such as steamboats, railroads, and machine guns, Western European nations could subdue peoples in Africa with the new technologies.

2. As a result, for the first time, many Europeans with superior military forces reached into the interior of Africa.

Test Tip

Be sure to study maps of imperialism in Africa and Asia circa 1914.

B. NATIONALISM

1. Nationalism—a sense of pride and devotion to one's country—was a powerful force in Europe and the Americas in the early 19th century. It was an important factor in empire building in this era. National pride was a cause of imperialism in two ways:

    i. Older European nations engaged in unofficial competitions to see who could grab the most territory around the world. It was a kind of rivalry. If Britain claimed *this*, then France wanted *that*, and on it went.

    ii. New nation-states such as Germany and Italy wanted to show that they belonged with the "Great Powers," so they got into the imperialism game as well. Britain's territories were so vast, they proudly boasted, "The sun never sets on the British Empire." By the end of this era, Britain's imperial possessions covered one-fourth of the Earth.

C. ECONOMICS

1. Controlling world markets was an objective harking back to the first round of European imperialism in the 16th and 17th centuries. (See the section on mercantilism in Chapter 7.) In this "new" imperialism, not only were governments and their treasuries involved, but also transnational corporations, such as the ones noted in the last chapter.

2. These corporations put pressure on governments to help them claim their "share" of the global economy. The economic stakes were greater because the amount and value of global trade was also greater.

3. Africa and Asia held vast amounts of raw materials that industrialized nations wanted to keep their economies booming, like cotton, rubber, and minerals. In addition, European imperialists saw Africa and Asia as great potential markets for their mass-produced goods like cloth and steel.

D. "THE WHITE MAN'S BURDEN"

1. This cause is tricky to define. The Europeans generally believed they were doing their "little brown brothers" of Africa, Asia, and Oceania (the Pacific Ocean region) a favor by conquering them. After all, they reasoned, the Europeans developed the inventions of the Industrial Revolution that made it possible to travel around the world. To many Europeans, bringing "them" technology, plus education, medicine, and Christianity was a noble cause.

2. The British writer of *The Jungle Book*, Rudyard Kipling, wrote a poem entitled "The White Man's Burden" about these ideas. This concept is strongly connected to Social Darwinism, explained below.

III. STATE EXPANSION FROM 1750 TO 1900

Before industrialization, Europe lacked the ability to move south of the Sahara Desert into Africa's interior. In the 16th century, the Portuguese set up some military outposts around South Africa's Cape of Good Hope and along the rim of the Indian Ocean, but did not establish any colonies. Within a hundred years, Europeans were transporting slaves from the Atlantic coast of Africa to the Americas but, again, did not establish colonies along West Africa's coast. The Dutch East India Company (the "VOC"—see Chapter 7) established a colony at Cape Town, South Africa in the mid-17th century and over the next hundred years, Dutch settlers established farms throughout the region.

A. EUROPEAN EXPANSION

1. In the early 1800s, British settlers moved to South Africa, causing strife with the Dutch colonists ("Boers")—as well as heightening tensions between the Dutch and the native Africans living there.

2. In the 1830s, France followed Britain's example and became a major African colonial power, first in Algeria and then across most of Northwest Africa.

3. Belgium began the infamous European "Scramble for Africa" in the 1880s by grabbing an enormous area in the "heart" of Africa—the Belgian Congo. When other European powers

realized Belgium had become a major colonial power, they began a rush to outdo each other in gaining territories.

4. The "Great Powers" of Europe met at the Berlin Conference of 1885 to divide Africa among themselves peacefully. Not invited to participate was anyone *from* Africa. Clearly, this led to problems. Europeans' confidence in their racial and cultural superiority did not leave much room for debate about the potential "down side" of imperialism. *Social Darwinism*—the theory that civilizations with superior technology and tactics *deserved* to conquer those without—was a powerful force in the West. By 1914, the sweep of European colonialism was so complete that only two areas in Africa were independent nations: Ethiopia (Italy tried, but failed, to colonize it in the late 19th century) and Liberia (founded as a colony for former American slaves).

5. Popular European literature with imperialist themes set in Africa included *Tarzan*, the story of a British boy raised by apes in the African jungle, and *Heart of Darkness*, a novel that criticized imperialist attitudes toward Africans.

B. IMPERIALISM IN ASIA AND THE PACIFIC

1. In contrast to their experiences in Africa, Europeans found that much of Asia could not be brought into their empires. The strength of Asian governments provided enough "pushback" to keep the Europeans at bay—the Ottoman Empire still had a formidable military force; Japan was becoming one of the major powers; and Europeans desired China's economic assets more than its land. France used a combination of military force and diplomacy to bring the Southeast Asia territory of Indo-China into its empire.

2. The greatest example of European imperialism in Asia was India, Britain's "jewel in the crown" of colonies. After the British won the Seven Years War against France in 1763, France lost control of most of its North American and South Asian holdings.

3. The British seized Canada and the eastern half of the future U.S. With significant help from the British East India Company (EIC), they established rule over South Asia. By the mid-19th century, the EIC had folded, and the British government began to exert direct control over its colony in South Asia and remained the colonial power there until 1947.

4. The British called their rule in India the *raj,* and Queen Victoria was named Empress of India. In addition, during the 19th century they extended colonial control to Malaysia and Singapore. Several islands in the Pacific and Indian Oceans were strategic refueling stations for British steam-powered military and cargo ships.

C. THE U.S., GERMANY, AND JAPAN BUILD EMPIRES

Three rising world powers in the mid-19th century had new, aggressive governments and strong national pride: the U.S., Germany, and Japan.

1. By the end of the 19th century, along with the other imperial powers, the U.S. began acquiring islands in the Pacific for strategic refueling bases. Spain's decline as a world power was sealed when it lost the Spanish-American War (1898–1901). As a result, the U.S. added the Philippines, Guam, and Puerto Rico to its colonial holdings. In addition, in 1898, the U.S. annexed Hawaii with its rich sugar plantations and vital port, Pearl Harbor.

2. Germany was established as a country only in the late 19th century, so it merits separate discussion. German leaders were determined to become a formidable power in Europe. In that era, international respect was granted to those with the most "toys," meaning colonies. At the Berlin Conference, Germany wrangled several African territories in strategic moves to counter British gains there. They also claimed some islands in the South Pacific.

3. After changing governments in the 1860s in the Meiji Restoration, Japan was eager to join Germany and the U.S. in establishing a place with the world's Great Powers. Japan began an aggressive campaign to create an empire in the Pacific region. Japan also wanted to counter Russian gains in East Asia. An early test of its new Western-style army was the Sino-Japanese war with China in the 1890s. Japan claimed Korea after its victory. Everyone, except Japan, was shocked when the Japanese defeated Russia in the Russo-Japanese War in 1905. The conflict was for control of territories in Manchuria and again, Korea.

D. EUROPEANS CREATED "WHITE DOMINIONS" AND "SETTLER COLONIES"

1. Britain developed "White Dominions," places where the English colonists, through disease and conquest, eventually outnumbered the native people. This occurred in Oceania (in Australia and New Zealand) and in North America in its American and Canadian colonies. "Settler colonies" were areas where Europeans settled and ruled, but remained a minority. South Africa and Singapore were two examples of British settler colonies, and the Philippines was a U.S. settler colony.

2. Algeria was a significant French settler colony in North Africa, where over 100,000 European colonists ruled over an Arab Muslim population of more than two million.

IV. INDIGENOUS RESPONSES TO STATE EXPANSION

A. Reactions of Africans to European imperialism ranged from warfare, to reluctant acceptance, to full cooperation. The French spent years subduing local rebellions in North Africa. The British battled Zulus and Dutch Boers in Southern Africa, and Muslims in Sudan. The Boer War left hundreds of thousands of casualties. At the end of the 19th century, descendants of Dutch settlers believed the newly arrived British were violating their property rights to land and slaves. In addition, they were angry about the gold and diamonds the British were hauling out of the territory once claimed by Boers.

1. Christian missionaries had some success spreading their faith in sub-Saharan Africa, but made no progress in the Muslim north. Europeans were determined to "civilize" the native population by dressing them in Western fashions and teaching them Western ways.

2. Other Africans signed treaties and acted as guides and interpreters for Europeans. Still others cooperated fully with the European powers. Often these were members of the African ruling elite families. They benefited financially and materially from working closely with the outsiders. Some were sent to Europe for full indoctrination into Western culture. After returning to their homelands, many of these elites began preparing independence movements.

3. Still other sub-Saharan Africans believed a spiritual movement would expel the foreigners. The Xhosa people in South Africa killed their cattle and burned their crops after a prophecy claimed that this would force the British to leave. After that, new cattle and crops would miraculously be restored to a revived Xhosa nation. Sadly, about 40,000 Xhosa people died of starvation.

B. REACTIONS BY ASIANS TO IMPERIALISM

1. In Asia, the same pattern emerged as in Africa: Some local people rebelled violently, while others tried to fit in to the colonial powers' ways of life. Military resistance to European occupation occurred in Afghanistan (against the British), the Philippines (against the U.S.) and in China, against foreigners in general. There, the Taiping and Boxer rebellions were highly anti-foreign in their nature.

2. In the mid-19th century in India, the "native" army, who were employed by the British colonial government and the East India Company, rebelled. It took British and pro-British Indian forces a year to suppress them. This resulted in the end of the Mughal dynasty which had ruled India since the 16th century, the dissolution of the East India Company, and the beginnings of the British *raj* over India.

3. Korea fought against French and later U.S. forces who sought trade agreements like those made with Japan and China.

4. There were also examples of cooperation. Many Indian soldiers remained loyal to the British in the Indian rebellion. The king of Siam (Thailand) decided to proactively deflect European colonization by inviting British representatives to help westernize his country.

Test Tip

The exam is fond of asking questions related to African and Asian responses to European imperialism.

V. GLOBAL ECONOMIC DEVELOPMENT IN THIS ERA

By the end of the 1800s, even those of modest means could buy goods from around the world. This was the result of rising incomes, faster and cheaper transportation, and more efficient production methods. For example, a Brazilian could purchase clothes made of Egyptian cotton, soap made of palm oil from West Africa, wheat from the U.S., tea from Ceylon, porcelain from China, meat from Argentina, and bananas from Honduras. Transnational corporations, like Lipton Tea, owned enormous plantations in South Asia and the crops were harvested by poorly paid workers. The tea was packed into steam-powered cargo ships for global markets.

VI. ECONOMIC IMPERIALISM, 1750–1900

You already know that imperialism had its political forms, and just learned about the rapidly expanding global economy, due to the Industrial Revolution. Economic imperialism was closely connected.

A. OPIUM WARS

The most infamous example of European economic imperialism in Asia was the Opium Wars pitting Britain and France against China in the mid-19th century. To offset huge trade deficits, the British smuggled opium from the Middle East and South Asia into China's ports, in defiance of Chinese laws. China's diplomatic protests went unheeded and war broke out between the two nations. Soon France joined Britain's side. China was overwhelmed and forced into a series of Unequal Treaties that increased the victors' economic presence, including ceding Hong Kong to British authority. Other nations, including Russia, Japan, and Germany eagerly negotiated their own Unequal Treaties with China.

B. Rather than colonization, these nations created "Spheres of Influence" within China, with each foreign nation having exclusive trading rights in "its" portion of China. As noted in Chapter 8, the U.S. proposed a trading free-for-all in China, called the Open Door Policy, which was accepted by the nations involved. China had little say in the matter.

C. See Chapter 8 to review economic imperialism as practiced in Latin America.

 ## VII. CAUSES OF MIGRATION IN A GLOBAL WORLD

In the era 1750–1900, faster transportation, an increased need for labor in the global economy, and violent unrest globally converged to create one of the greatest ages of human migration. As the Industrial Revolution spread, more people took engine-powered ships and trains to new destinations. These migrations occurred within Afro-Eurasia and within the Americas, but it was the migrations to North and South America *from* Afro-Eurasia that historians focus on in this era.

Migrations have two overarching causes: "push" factors that make people want to leave their home, and "pull" factors that draw them to a different location.

A. PUSH FACTORS

1. Population pressures. The Industrial Revolution brought new technology, new kinds of fertilizers to farms (meaning more food), and new medicines. These combined—and continue to combine—to increase populations and allow longer life spans. India, China, and Japan were demographic centers of this push factor toward the Americas and points in the Pacific region. People with the ability to do so often left these regions for less populated ones.

2. Faster and cheaper transportation. It wasn't luxurious, but reliable steamship transportation across the oceans was cheap enough for most—provided they could reach a port city.

3. Political unrest and religious persecution. The revolutions throughout the world in the 19th century caused political instability and were a major push factor for migrants to leave their homelands. An additional push factor was religious persecutions, such as the anti-Jewish pogroms in Russia.

4. Famine. Along with the Irish famine of the mid-19th century, other famines pushed people away from East and South Asia.

B. PULL FACTORS

1. Urbanization. Migrants gravitated to cities with people of the same heritage. Italian, Jewish, German, and Chinese neighborhoods developed. In addition, more government services were offered to migrants in cities than in rural areas.

2. Farmland. The U.S., Canada, Russia, and many Latin American nations encouraged immigration with generous land policies. For example, the U.S. offered 160 acres of farmland in the Western Great Plains to settlers who worked their tract of land for five years.

3. Abolition of slavery. The end of slavery in the Western world by the late 19th century did not end the need for agricultural labor. Indentured labor, a situation in which one signs on to be—for all intents and purposes—a "temporary slave," with release from obligation after a period—from 5 to 10 years— was a strong pull factor for migrants from South and East Asia. Indentured servants worked on sugar plantations in the Caribbean into the 1920s, and were a significant source of labor on islands in the Indian Ocean and in South Africa.

4. Economic opportunity. Many nations, especially in the Americas, offered opportunities for economic advancement that were impossible elsewhere. Discoveries of gold in Australia, Alaska, and northwest Canada triggered "rushes" of migrants into those areas.

5. Political and religious freedom. Pushed out by revolutions and persecutions, migrants sought new lands hoping for greater political participation and religious tolerance. Many Southern Europeans and Germans migrated to South and North America, while migrants from North Africa sought opportunities in Europe.

The AP® World History: Modern exam is known for questions related to migration in general and the causes and effects of migration in the industrial era in particular.

VIII. EFFECTS OF MIGRATIONS

A. CHANGES IN DEMOGRAPHICS

1. Massive migrations changed the demographics in areas receiving immigrants, but what about the effects on places that lost population? In Africa, European powers promoted large-scale, single-crop farming for export. Huge numbers of male workers left their homelands and migrated to large farming areas, and other men sought job opportunities in Africa's larger cities.

2. Women coped by taking on responsibilities that had once been primarily "man's work," such as trade, growing crops for home use, and mining.

3. Another example: about 2 million Italians migrated to Argentina from the late 19th through the early 20th centuries.

B. RESENTMENT AGAINST MIGRANTS

1. With the influx of migrants came resistance from many who had established themselves previously in the "receiving" lands.

2. Besides personal prejudices, legal restrictions on migrations also appeared, such as the 1882 Chinese Exclusion Act in the U.S. and the White Australian Act of 1901.

C. SAMPLE POPULATION SHIFTS

1. Through the 19th century and into the early 20th, about 60 million people migrated from Europe; most settled in the Americas, about 30 million of them in the U.S.

2. About 2.5 million people left China between 1850 and 1900; most went to the U.S. and the western side of South America.

3. About 45 million people migrated from South Asia to Southeast Asia, along the Indian Ocean region and into the South Pacific, Southern Africa, and the Caribbean.

4. Roughly 50 million people left western Russia and northeast Asia for Japan, Manchuria, Siberia, and Central Asia.

Use Chapter 9 to develop your causation reasoning processes. The DBQ and Long Essay require you to analyze ("this happened because. . . .") your evidence. The AP® World History: Modern reasoning processes (Continuity-and-Change-Over-Time, Comparison, and Causation) are featured mainly in the writing parts of the exam.

➤ To test yourself on causation in this unit, rank the causes of migration from most to least significant and defend your choices: Why is that cause the greatest? Why did you choose your least significant cause? Do the same with effects of migration. See Chapters 19 and 20 to delve into writing DBQs and LEQs.

UNIT 7

Global Conflict

c. 1900 to the Present

Some historians regard the two world wars as one event with a pause in between. Other major European wars had similar patterns: Nations fighting the Hundred Years War and the Thirty Years War took long "time-outs" between hostilities. The Cold War followed World War II and threatened global nuclear war.

I. SHIFTING POWER AFTER 1900

The 20th century began with European empires in control around the globe. The Western mindset would assume things would stay that way. In 1900, the U.S. and Japan were rising powers, while Russia and China were crumbling from within. By the end of the 20th century, after two world wars and a global "Cold War," European hegemony (control) had declined dramatically, and China's power was rapidly on the rise. In between those historical bookends, European colonies around the world gained independence, and Russia became the first of many communist nations. After World War II, Russia, now called the Union of Soviet Socialist Republics (USSR), and the United States led their allies through decades of global tensions. By 2000, Cold War worries had faded, but new challenges to political, social, and economic stability emerged.

A. OLDER, DECLINING POWERS

1. Both Spain and Portugal saw their empires dwindle because of successful independence movements in Latin America against their rule. In addition, Spain's defeat in the Spanish-American War in 1898 effectively marked the end of that empire and the rise of the U.S. on the global stage.

2. While many European neighbors were "going global" during the Age of Imperialism, the Ottoman Empire was shrinking.

Beginning with the successful nationalistic Greek rebellion for independence in the 1820s, it lost territories in the Balkan Peninsula in Eastern Europe and faced growing opposition in its Arab holdings in Southwest Asia and North Africa. In addition, Russia and Britain fought the Crimean War over the Ottoman Empire's vital Bosporus and Dardanelles sea lanes near Constantinople. While the Empire came out on the winning side with its British and French allies against Russia, it remained a weakened "Sick Man of Europe" and by the early 20th century sought alliances in an attempt to hang on.

3. The Russian Empire declined in the 19th century even though it stretched across more territory than any other empire in the world. Attempts to overthrow the czar led to some reforms like freeing the serfs but also increased government oppression of opponents, mostly socialists and communists. In 1905, Russia shockingly lost a war with Japan, triggering a revolt that further reduced the czar's power.

4. Qing China began the 19th century as the world's top economy, but began declining after the Opium Wars with Britain and France. Weak leaders, a civil war, famine, and a refusal to commit to industrialization pushed China into disarray by 1900.

5. The Austrian Empire, a major European power in the early 19th century, fragmented into many groups, based on ethnicity.

6. Last-ditch attempts by these failing empires to maintain power produced tensions that led to World War I.

B. THE MEXICAN REVOLUTION

1. The Mexican Revolution of the early 20th century saw great political and social upheaval, including a long civil war. The result was a new constitution that promised free public education, land reform, and the reduced influence of the Catholic Church.

2. Mexico nationalized its oil reserves and production from foreign control in 1938.

3. Women were granted the vote ("franchise") in the 1950s.

II. CAUSES OF WORLD WAR I

A. OUTBREAK OF WORLD WAR I

The event that sparked World War I was the tragic, but seemingly inconsequential, assassination of the future emperor of Austria-Hungary. A chain of reactions to the assassination led to a realignment of the alliances into the "Allies," initially Britain, France, Russia, and Italy, and the "Central Powers," Germany, Austria-Hungary, and the Ottoman Empire.

B. CAUSES OF WORLD WAR I INCLUDED:

1. Failing Empires (discussed earlier)

2. Imperialism. The colonial powers of Europe had competed for decades over land in Africa and Asia. Early in the 20th century, wrangling continued over ever-diminishing amounts of unclaimed territories.

3. Nationalism. Tensions rose inside empires like Austria-Hungary, the Ottoman Empire, and Russia from ethnic groups that wanted to break off and form their own nations.

4. Arms races. The Industrial Revolution mass-produced weapons that could kill at faster rates, and from longer distances, than ever before. National pride among the "Great Powers" of Europe started an unofficial competition between governments to see which could produce the best weapons. Eventually, they decided to try them out on each other.

5. Alliance system. Rather than risking going to war alone, the Great Powers formed two competing military alliances in the early 20th century: Russia, Britain, and France formed the Triple Entente and Germany, Italy, and Austria-Hungary formed the Triple Alliance. Geographically, the Entente was positioned on Germany's eastern and western borders.

6. All of these factors led to heightened tensions in Europe by 1914. A chain reaction to the assassination of Archduke Ferdinand led to a realignment of the alliances into the "Allies," initially Britain, France, Russia, and Italy, and the "Central Powers" of Germany, Austria-Hungary, and the Ottoman Empire.

C. POSTWAR LEAGUE OF NATIONS

Survivors prayed that World War I would indeed be the "war to end all wars." No previous conflict had caused as much widespread destruction of lives, property, and empires. The creation of a global League of Nations at the war's end in 1918, designed to keep the peace, gave many people hope that governments and individuals had learned their lesson. Their hopes were short-lived.

 III. CONDUCTING WORLD WAR I

No one expected a long war—especially Germany, which attacked France and Russia simultaneously, anticipating a restoration of stability in Europe with a German flavor. When that did not occur, the two sides hunkered down into defensive positions in France (the Western Front) and Russia (the Eastern Front) by the end of 1914. By 1915, fighting spread to the Ottoman Empire and the European colonies in Africa.

A. New weapons of World War I—the machine gun, poison gas, the airplane and the submarine to name a few—led to changes in tactics and philosophy about war itself. The Industrial Revolution showed its ugly side by producing weapons of mass destruction. The machine gun forced combatants into defensive trenches, but despite the gun's tactical advantage, military leaders sent long lines of men to charge across open fields called "no man's land."

1. The result was a tremendous loss of life, which had the unintended consequence of lowering the value of humanity in war. Thus, all civilians became legitimate targets in "total war"—where the full economic and political power of nations was engaged in military victory. Women replaced men in factories in large numbers.

2. Submarines torpedoed enemy civilian and military ships and airplanes bombed cities. Air warfare had even greater consequences in World War II.

B. USE OF COLONIAL SOLDIERS

European colonization resulted in recruiting soldiers from Africa and Asia to fight. India, for example, committed one million troops to aid the British forces.

1. Canada, South Africa, Australia, and New Zealand, autonomous members of the British Empire, also sent hundreds of thousands of troops to support the Allies' cause.

2. The British also convinced Arabs to fight the Ottoman Empire in Southwest Asia with Arab independence from the Ottomans as a reward.

C. USE OF PROPAGANDA

Both the Allied and the Central Powers used government-produced posters, advertisements, and even movies to stir patriotism for their side and hatred for their enemies.

D. END OF WORLD WAR I

In 1917, the U.S. entered World War I on the Allies' side "to make the world safe for democracy," according to U.S. President Woodrow Wilson. By late 1918, the Central Powers had run out of human resources to wage war, and an armistice was signed. The U.S. proposed the Fourteen Points Plan, which was designed to stop future wars. The key component was an international organization—the League of Nations—formed to settle differences between member nations in order to avoid war.

1. The Russian, Austrian, Ottoman, and German empires dissolved. Two Allied nations, the U.S. and Japan, emerged with their industrial capacity and colonial possessions intact, unlike most of Europe.

2. Conducting the war amid rising internal unrest was too great for the Russian czar's government. In 1917, it collapsed and was replaced by a provisional democracy. But the new government quickly fell to a communist uprising. Bolshevik leader Vladimir Lenin negotiated an early withdrawal from the war with the German government. (Details of the rise of the world's first communist regime are covered later in this chapter.)

3. Arming colonial subjects to support Europe's war effort was shortsighted. Nationalist leaders in African and Asian colonies used their experience in military training to revolt in the years after World War I. In addition, many elites had learned about European ideals, such as self-rule, while attending European schools. Another encouragement for leaders of colonial independence movements was found in a key feature of the Fourteen Points Plan—a call for "self-determination" for nationalist groups.

IV. THE ECONOMY IN THE INTERWAR PERIOD (1919–1938)

A. GREAT DEPRESSION

The end of World War I brought great optimism that future wars would be impossible. Most survivors also thought that riches were just around the corner. Unfortunately, the closely connected global economy began to fail for many European nations after World War I.

1. The U.S. economy, the world's strongest, collapsed at the end of the "Roaring Twenties," further damaging the world's markets in the global Great Depression.

   i. As a result, the industrialized nations reorganized their governments to be more active in financial matters, including government programs of social security, unemployment compensation, bank regulation, and many others. Italy, Germany, and Japan were prominent in radically changing their governmental and financial systems to address the economic crisis.

B. COMMUNISM

Even before the Great Depression, Russia withdrew from the Allies during World War I because of lack of progress on the Eastern Front and civil strife in the cities, especially in the capital of Petrograd (previously called St. Petersburg). In 1917, the czar resigned and within six months, a communist revolution began. A civil war ended in 1922 with the communists victorious.

1. For the next several years, leaders consolidated power, ruthlessly killing many real and imagined enemies. High priority was given to military modernization.

2. The new communist government set up Five-Year Plans for economic goals for the command economy (planned and directed by the government).

3. Many historians believe that policy insulated the USSR from the Great Depression. However, during that time the Soviet Union's leaders—in particular the dictator Stalin—were committing mass atrocities against their people.

C. FASCISM

Italy was disgruntled by the Treaty of Versailles because it did not gain as many benefits as its allies, Britain and France. In 1922, the democratic government was overthrown and replaced by leaders who promoted fascism.

1. Fascist ideology claimed to solve the failures of capitalism and the extreme policies of communism. The government formed coalitions with banks and industries, eventually taking charge of most of the economy. Many public works programs like dam-building and upgrading railroads were undertaken. Modernization of the military had high importance.

2. As in the USSR, dissent was brutally crushed by Italy's dictator, Mussolini.

3. Fascism seemed to work to outsiders who didn't look too closely, and gained popularity in Western Europe, especially in Germany and Japan.

4. Germany's unstable economy and government after World War I made it ripe for radical change. Hitler inspired the masses with promises while killing opponents more to the left (communists) and on the right (the Weimar Republic). By 1934, Hitler had declared himself the unquestioned dictator of National Socialist (Nazi) Germany.

D. THE NEW DEAL AND SIMILAR PROGRAMS

1. The U.S. government dealt with the Great Depression with the New Deal, which involved higher taxes on the wealthy, deficit spending, massive public works programs, and social welfare

policies. Britain and France attempted similar programs, but with fewer resources they continued to struggle economically.

V. UNRESOLVED TENSIONS AFTER WORLD WAR I

World War I ended with many issues unresolved: What to do with European colonies around the world? How to slow the spread of military technology? How to deal with colonial nationalist movements? What to do about a new communist Russian nation and how to recover from the economic, political, and social damage of World War I? About 20 million soldiers and civilians died in the war, which was fought predominantly in Europe, but also in Southwest Asia and Africa. The political, social, and economic impact of the loss of so many people shaped many Europeans' attitudes about war for the next two decades.

A. THE TREATY OF VERSAILLES

1. Ended World War I

2. Formed out of the Fourteen Points

3. Created the League of Nations, but also dictated terms to the Central Powers focused on punishing Germany. Many Germans strongly resented the victorious Allied nations, especially after their economy imploded due to the harsh reparation demands from Britain and France. Many vengeful Germans sought alternatives to the new democracy imposed by the Allies.

4. Although the U.S. proposed the formation of the League of Nations, it was never a member, thus contributing to the League's limitations and ultimate failure.

B. INTERNATIONAL TREATIES

1. Between the world wars, international treaties sought to limit the expansion of military might, and thus reduce the chance of war.

2. The Five Power Treaty, the London Naval Conference of 1930, and the Kellogg-Briand Pact were the most important.

C. MANDATE SYSTEM

1. The African, Asian, and Pacific colonies of Germany and the Ottoman Empire were taken by the League of Nations and redistributed among the victors, especially France and Britain, who set up a mandate system.

2. The League decided that those colonies weren't ready for independence, so they would be governed by Britain, France, or some other ally.

3. This policy only fueled nationalist feelings among the Arab provinces of the Ottomans (like Syria and Jordan) and the Europeans' African colonies.

D. "GREATER EAST ASIA CO-PROSPERITY SPHERE"

1. Between the wars, Japan extended its control over East and Southeast Asia, creating the "Greater East Asia Co-Prosperity Sphere," which it professed would liberate these regions from Western oppression. In reality, Japan exploited member nations like Thailand and Burma for their own economic gain. The best-known member of the Sphere was Manchukuo, in northeast China and Manchuria. Many people in this "puppet state" were practically enslaved to serve the Japanese empire.

E. INDIAN NATIONAL CONGRESS

1. By far the most important example of resistance to European colonialism in this era was the Indian National Congress, which formed in the late 19th century.

F. WOMEN'S SUFFRAGE

1. Women made political gains in the U.S. and Britain after World War I when they won the right to vote (suffrage).

VI. CAUSES OF WORLD WAR II

Primarily a continuation of unresolved issues from World War I, World War II outdid its predecessor in duration, global scope, use of military technology, and death.

UNIT 7 | c. 1900 to the Present

A. The Treaty of Versailles, discussed previously, required Germany to accept full guilt for the war, reduce its military forces, hand over its colonies and pay billions in war reparations to Britain and France. These humiliations left many Germans seeking vengeance.

B. **TOTALITARIAN REGIMES**

Fascism required conquest to obtain cheap labor and raw material.

1. Italy invaded North Africa and Ethiopia in the 1930s, Germany invaded Czechoslovakia and Austria at about the same time.

2. Japan overran its neighbors even before it officially turned to fascism. Some historians argue that World War II really started in 1931 when Japan subdued Manchuria, killed or enslaved its peoples, and occupied their coal mines and factories. Not satisfied, Japan invaded China in 1937.

3. Spain also became a fascist dictatorship in the 1930s, but had a much less aggressive foreign policy.

4. Germany aggressively moved on its neighbors to the east during the 1930s, annexing Czechoslovakia and Austria.

C. **APPEASEMENT**

The well-intentioned but weak leaders in Britain and France, and the League of Nations could not stop aggression by Italy, Germany, and Japan in the 1930s. Europe's democracies hoped that fascists would be appeased after limited conquests and seek no more territory.

1. This policy of *appeasement* only encouraged the attackers who showed no respect for the League's hopes for peace.

2. After World War II, the U.S. and USSR rejected appeasement in favor of "peace through strength."

D. **EFFECTS OF THE GREAT DEPRESSION**

The weak economies in Britain and France after World War I left their governments looking inward for the most part, generally little interested in the aggressive actions of Germany, Spain, Italy, and Japan.

VII. CONDUCTING WORLD WAR II

A. AXIS vs. ALLIES

1. As in World War I, there were two alliances in World War II: the Allies and the Axis Powers. The Axis remained constant. The Allies grew in number as they came under attack by Axis nations. Germany, Italy, and Japan formed the Axis. Britain, France, and most of Western Europe formed the Allies by 1940. A year later, the USSR and the U.S. joined the Allies.

B. WAR TECHNOLOGY

Unlike World War I, which featured defensive fighting like trench warfare, World War II saw fast-moving fronts.

1. Technology improved the machines that were introduced in World War I. Tanks and airplanes moved much faster by the 1930s and defensive trenches were impractical.

2. Germany introduced the new tactic of *blitzkrieg*, which involved massive bombing by airplanes, rapid advances of tanks and waves of soldiers, all designed to quickly overwhelm the enemy—which was most of Europe.

C. TOTAL WAR

As in World War I, but on a much bigger scale, governments used the media to promote the war through propaganda such as patriotic movies, posters, and radio broadcasts.

1. Civilians in enemy countries were often considered equal targets as soldiers. Massive bombing campaigns by air killed millions of them in Europe and Asia.

2. Even in Western democracies, governments directed factory production, rationed food and goods, and rounded up dissenters.

3. The USSR and the Axis Powers killed many alleged spies and war opponents.

D. SCOPE OF WORLD WAR II

World War II's battlefields were on a more global scale. The Pacific theater was added to those in Europe and Africa.

UNIT 7 | c. 1900 to the Present

1. Europe. The war officially started in 1939 when Germany invaded Poland. In 1938, Britain had appeased the German fascist dictator Hitler in his conquest of central Europe, but drew a line at Poland. After war was declared, Germany swiftly conquered most of Western Europe, including France by 1940. Russia and Germany completed a peace treaty in 1939, so Britain faced Nazi aggression alone.

2. Two significant events in 1941 turned the tide against Nazi Germany: Hitler's surprise invasion of Russia went poorly for Germany, and the U.S. entered the war against the Axis Powers after Japan attacked Pearl Harbor.

3. Unlike in World War I, Russia stayed with the Allies to the end of the war, despite suffering perhaps 25 million deaths.

4. The turning point of the war was the Allied invasion of France in 1944. By May 1945, Allies had pressed Germany from the east (USSR) and west (U.S., Britain, France) to force an unconditional surrender.

5. North Africa. The first Allied offensive against the Axis powers was in North Africa. From there, the Allies pushed into Italy to put pressure on the Axis.

6. Asia and the Pacific

   i. Japan attacked much of Southeast Asia and islands throughout the Pacific in conjunction with its attack on Hawaii's Pearl Harbor in 1941.

   ii. The U.S. entered the Pacific war and, with Britain as its main ally, slowly pushed the Japanese empire's perimeter back toward their homeland.

   iii. In August 1945, the U.S. dropped two atomic bombs on Japan and ended World War II. Japan's campaign in China was particularly brutal, causing about 20 million deaths.

7. Allied Victory. The unwavering commitment to victory from Britain's prime minister, Winston Churchill, the U.S. president Franklin Roosevelt, and the USSR's general secretary Josef Stalin was a major factor in the Allies' success.

E. CASUALTIES IN WORLD WAR II

1. An estimated 60 million people died in the war. Whole cities were destroyed in Germany and Japan.

2. In Europe, including the USSR, and in Asia, especially Japan and China, infrastructure and the economy were in ruins.

VIII. MASS ATROCITIES AFTER 1900

Some governments attempted to exterminate groups of people deemed unworthy to live.

A. ARMENIAN GENOCIDE

Starting in 1915, the Ottoman Empire launched a campaign labeled "Turkey for the Turks" against the Christian Armenian minority, killing about 1.5 million people and exiling many others. Survivors scattered to many countries, including Russia and the U.S.

B. UKRAINIAN GENOCIDE

Early under communist rule in the USSR, peasant farmers were granted small plots of land and cattle to raise. Stalin changed the policy, collectivizing huge tracts of farmland and requiring farmers to meet government requisitions for produce. Farmers in Ukraine (a large state in the USSR) revolted, and Stalin retaliated by hauling away what food there was, leaving the farm families to starve to death in what is known as the Artificial Famine of 1932–33. Others were hauled to gulags (prison camps); still others were shot. About 10 million died.

C. THE JEWISH HOLOCAUST

Central to Nazi philosophy was holding Jews responsible for the world's problems throughout history. Hitler preached about creating a pure "Aryan" German nation, free from Jews and others he thought undesirable. Beginning with denying Jews civil rights, continuing with forcing them into "ghettos" (areas of town where Jews had to live), later imprisonment in concentration camps and ending with the "final solution" of death, 6 million of Europe's 9 million Jews were executed.

D. CAMBODIAN GENOCIDE

In the late 1970s, the radical communist government in Cambodia—the Khmer Rouge—set out to purge the nation of all ethnic and religious minorities and suspected political opponents. About 2 million of Cambodia's 8 million people were murdered.

IX. CAUSATION IN GLOBAL CONFLICT

Practice your arguing skills for the exam by addressing this question:

What causes governments to go to war on a global scale?

This chapter discusses many factors, including the three below. Rapid changes in population due to massive migrations, improved medicine, and greater food production (due to improved fertilizers and mechanization of farms) led to social, political, environmental, and economic strains. These tensions contributed to the other factors you learned about in this chapter that led to two world wars in the 20th century. Three of these factors are:

A. FAILING EMPIRES

B. CHALLENGES TO THE EXISTING ORDER

C. IMPROVED MILITARY TECHNOLOGY

Review this chapter and place the causes of World War I and World War II under each of the three categories above. Next, rank your choices from the greatest to least cause. Defend your choice for greatest cause with specific examples.

Now, drill down a little more. Which of the outcomes (that is, effects) of World War I was the greatest cause of World War II? Defend your answer.

Test Tip

Remember, causation has two sides: causes and effects of historical processes.

UNIT 8

Cold War and Decolonization

c. 1900 to the Present

The United Nations (UN) replaced the League of Nations after World War II. Two key differences stood out: the UN's headquarters was in the U.S., not Europe—a sign of America's postwar influence—and, unlike the League, the UN had military power it could use to stop aggression by nations.

Western Europe's reign as the world's strongest economic and political force ended with World War II. Two devastating wars crippled Europe, while the U.S. was the only major power whose economy and society remained strong. One by one, aided by the UN, Europe's colonies in Africa and Asia gained independence.

 SETTING THE STAGE FOR THE COLD WAR AND DECOLONIZATION

A. CAUSES OF THE COLD WAR

1. The Yalta Conference. Near the end of the World War II, the Allies met to redraw the maps of Europe and Asia for the post-war world. Germany and its capital, Berlin, were divided into Western and Soviet regions. The USSR took control of most of Eastern Europe, promising those countries self-determination. When that pledge failed to materialize, the West discounted Soviet guarantees and intentions, and, as the world's only communist nation in 1945, the USSR suspected its old allies were out to destroy it.

2. The Yalta Conference also divided Korea into communist north and capitalist south nations. Japan was put into the U.S. sphere of influence. The U.S. replaced Japan's government with a democratic constitutional monarchy.

An important skill to learn is how to discuss "context"— setting the stage for an event or process in the time in which it happened.

II. THE COLD WAR

If anything approached "World War III," it was the Cold War. The capitalist U.S. and its Western allies competed with the communist USSR and its allies for global superiority. What made it a "cold" war was that the main antagonists did not fight each other directly on a battlefield. However, everything else involved in a "hot" war was in play: threats of destruction, the gathering of military allies, arms build-ups, spy networks, and propaganda campaigns. Even the exploration of space and Olympic competitions were part of the Cold War. The addition of nuclear weapons made the outcome of any such war extremely hazardous to the entire world.

Some early events in the Cold War included:

A. THE BERLIN AIRLIFT

1. In 1946, the USSR attempted to cut off Western access to Berlin, which was in Soviet-controlled East Germany. For a year, the U.S. and Britain flew supplies into the Western sector of Berlin. The Soviets realized the futility of their blockade and lifted it. This event increased Cold War tensions between the two sides. In 1961, communist East Germany built a wall dividing the pro-West sector of Berlin from its communist half. The Berlin Wall was finally torn down in 1989.

B. THE MARSHALL PLAN

1. To help its Western European allies recover from the war, the U.S. sent billions of dollars in economic and construction aid to West Germany, Britain, France, and other nations. Japan also received massive amounts of reconstruction assistance. The USSR provided a similar but less successful aid package for Eastern Europe called Comecon.

EFFECTS OF THE COLD WAR

A. THE USSR DEVELOPED NUCLEAR WEAPONS A FEW YEARS AFTER WORLD WAR II

This disturbed the Western allies, but the Soviet Union claimed they were for self-defense.

B. NATO vs. THE WARSAW PACT

1. In 1949, the U.S. formed an alliance with Western European nations designed to deter Soviet aggression in Europe. Canada and Turkey were included. The USSR responded with a military alliance of its own, the Warsaw Pact, which included most Eastern European nations. For decades, most experts assumed World War III would be fought in Central Europe between these two sides.

C. CHINESE COMMUNIST LEADER MAO ZEDONG SEIZED CONTROL OF CHINA IN 1949

1. The 20th century Chinese Revolutions and China's Cold War relationship with the USSR and the West are discussed later in this chapter.

D. LATIN AMERICA

1. Cold War tensions peaked during the Cuban Missile Crisis in 1962. Cuba became a communist nation in 1959, and the USSR secretly placed missiles with nuclear capabilities there. The U.S. discovered the missiles and brought the issue to the UN. Before a nuclear exchange of missiles occurred, cooler heads prevailed. In Central America in the late 1970s and early 1980s, guerilla wars between pro- and anti-communist forces involved U.S. and Soviet funding, weapons, and "advisors."

E. NON-ALIGNED NATIONS

1. Most nations sided with either the U.S. or the USSR. This political reality was called "Bi-Polarism." However, some nations claimed not to pick sides and called themselves the Non-Aligned Nations. Key members of the non-aligned group were Indonesia and its leader, Sukarno, India and its leader, Nehru,

Kenya and its leader, Nkrumah, and Yugoslavia and its leader, Tito.

F. PROXY WARS

1. The main Cold War powers—the U.S. and the USSR—fought "proxy wars" in third world countries to spread their ideologies. In these wars the two superpowers did not fight each other directly, but provided materiel and funding to pro- and anti-communist regimes. Examples include Korea and Vietnam and Angola.

IV. SPREAD OF COMMUNISM AFTER 1900

A. REVOLUTIONS IN CHINA LED TO COMMUNIST RULE

1. The Qing dynasty ended in 1911 and was not replaced by a new imperial dynasty. This event marked the end of thousands of years of dynastic rule in China.

2. The new government was the Republic of China, promoted by Sun Yat-sen (Sun Yi Xian), a Western-educated member of the Chinese elite. Sun struggled to create a stable, unified China and accepted foreign aid, especially from the new Soviet Union.

3. Sun died in 1925 and was replaced by Chiang Kai-Shek (Jiang Jieshî). Unlike Sun, Chiang vigorously opposed cooperation with communists. Under Chiang, the Nationalist-led republic was perceived as massively corrupt and had little support among the peasants. Regions in China fell into civil war between communists and Nationalists supporting the Republic.

4. When Japan invaded China in 1937, the communists and Nationalists united to fight their common enemy. At the end of World War II, China's civil war restarted and, in 1949, the communists, led by Mao Zedong, won. The Nationalist government, still supported by Western powers, fled to Taiwan, an island nation near mainland China.

5. Mao's government officially granted full rights to women, which was a radical departure from China's history.

6. China supported North Korea in the Korean War, sending millions of soldiers into battle.

7. In the late 1950s, Mao pushed a "Great Leap Forward" program that promoted industrial output over agricultural production. The result was a catastrophe that killed as many as 20 million people by starvation. Mao's response was to blame capitalist influences that allegedly remained in China. So the "Cultural Revolution" was enacted to purge all vestiges of Western culture. A decade of government persecutions and re-education centers finally ended with Mao's death in 1976.

8. By the 1960s, two nations that might appear to be natural allies were enemies: the USSR and communist China. They fought over territories on their mutual borders and did little to support each other in spreading communism around the globe.

B. THE KOREAN WAR

1. At the end of World War II, the USSR and the U.S. agreed to divide Korea into a communist north and pro-West south. In 1950, North Korea invaded South Korea and, for the first time, the UN sent soldiers from member nations to push out the aggressor. The U.S. led the UN forces that included a massive surge from communist Chinese soldiers into Korea. After three years, the boundaries of the two Koreas were established near their previous borders. The U.S. and its military allies announced a global plan of "containment" designed to keep communism from spreading beyond its 1950 borders.

C. THE VIETNAM WAR

1. Just after World War II, a war for independence in French colonial Indochina became a Cold War battle for that region. It was divided in the early 1950s into four nations, including pro-communist North Vietnam—led by Ho Chi Min—and pro-West South Vietnam. Much like in Korea, North Vietnam soon invaded South Vietnam to unify the country under communist rule. Vietnam became the focus of U.S. containment policy. The U.S. committed its army to fighting a limited war until the communists of North Vietnam defeated and absorbed South Vietnam in 1975. Hundreds of thousands of South Vietnamese migrated to France, Australia, and the U.S. over the next two decades.

V. DECOLONIZATION AFTER 1900

Europe was weakened after two world wars. Europe's decline as a world power was typified by successful colonial independence movements after World War II. Some colonies gained independence peacefully, others by violent revolutions. By the mid-1970s, almost all former European colonies returned to local control. Decolonization became one of the major themes of the 20th century.

A. ASIA

1. The first major colony to gain independence after World War II was also the largest. Mohandas Gandhi led non-violent resistance to the British *raj* for decades, supported by the Indian National Congress and the Muslim League. Their efforts were successful in 1947, but Gandhi's dream of a united, independent India was not fulfilled. In South Asia, the Muslim League used religion as an additional factor in seeking independence. Muslim-majority areas, such as Pakistan and Bangladesh, formed separate nations in what was known as the Partition of India. However, ethnic violence occurred after independence when Hindus and Muslims clashed near the India-Pakistan border and an estimated one million died.

2. The Dutch East Indies and Indochina represent two colonies that rebelled violently for independence. The Netherlands granted independence to the new nation of Indonesia in 1965. As discussed earlier, France granted independence after Indochina split into four nations: Laos, Cambodia, and North and South Vietnam.

3. Hong Kong did not gain independence, but the British peacefully transferred sovereignty of Hong Kong—which it had held since the Opium Wars—to communist China in 1997 on the promise that the island would remain a capitalist haven.

B. AFRICA

1. North African nations tended to gain independence from European control earlier than sub-Saharan nations. In the 1950s, the UN supported the peaceful independence of Libya and Tunisia from French rule. The most significant rebellion in North Africa occurred in Algeria, where French soldiers battled nationalist rebels until France granted independence in 1962.

2. Ghana was the first sub-Saharan colony to gain independence, peacefully, in 1957. However, in Angola, rebels aided by the USSR, China, and Cuba, fought against Portuguese rule until becoming independent in 1975. Most other African colonies gained freedom through peaceful means and with support from the UN.

C. LATIN AMERICA

In Latin America, Europe's few colonies gained independence in the postwar era as well. The Bahamas and the Guiana colonies in South America are two examples.

VI. NEWLY INDEPENDENT STATES

Some former colonies had economic success and political stability after decolonization, including India, Singapore, and Indonesia. However, many colonies struggled, facing civil wars, crumbling infrastructure, and continued economic dependence on their old colonial rulers.

1. Malawi and Zaire are two examples in Africa of the latter, but there are many more. A continuity over the centuries has been Africa's lack of industrial production. It remains an exporter primarily of natural resources such as oil, gold, and other minerals.

   i. Palestine/Israel. After World War I, Britain had a mandate over Palestine that lasted just after World War II. In 1947, the UN called for a partition of Palestine into Jewish-majority and Arab-majority states. A year later, the U.S. recognized the state of Israel, but the Palestinian question remained unresolved.

   ii. Some newly independent states in Asia and Africa used their governments to direct economic modernization, with mixed results. India's prime minister Indira Gandhi enacted emergency powers to, she claimed, end poverty there. Egypt's government funded flood control of the Nile River, nationalized (government control of) about half of the country's businesses, but most Egyptians remained in poverty.

   iii. Perhaps because of slow economic and social progress in the new nations, many people from Asia and Africa migrated to their former colonial countries. Pakistanis and Indians moved to Britain in large numbers; Algerians flocked to France and Filipinos migrated to the U.S., which had colonized the Philippines for fifty years.

iv. Massive internal migration in the new nations in Africa and Asia led to mega-cities like Lagos, Nigeria (population: 21 million) and Karachi, Pakistan (population: 15 million).

VII. GLOBAL RESISTANCE TO ESTABLISHED POWER STRUCTURES AFTER 1900

A. END OF APARTHEID

South Africa was part of the British Empire, but wasn't a colony per se. It became an independent country in 1910, but retained strong political and economic ties to Britain, like Canada and Australia. South Africa had a long-standing policy of white minority rule: *apartheid*. Whites of Dutch, German, and British descent had full political rights, but the majority black population and mixed-race peoples had none for most of the 20th century. A movement demanding majority rule, led by Nelson Mandela, eventually forced the government to yield to increasing international pressure and transitioned to constitutional rights for all citizens, regardless of color, in the 1990s.

B. END OF SEGREGATION IN THE U.S.

Dr. Martin Luther King, Jr., was inspired by Mohandas Gandhi's non-violent passive resistance campaigns in India, and used similar methods to call for economic and social justice in the U.S. Racial violence flared in many cities from the 1950s to early 1970s, but his goals of fair treatment in jobs, housing, and voting were largely achieved.

C. VIOLENCE IN RESPONSE TO CHANGE

Some governments responded to calls for reform in their countries with violence.

1. Spain's fascist dictator Franco repressed political opponents for more than thirty years. Historians estimate that as many as 300,000 people were put in concentration camps or executed.

2. In Chile, the dictator Pinochet persecuted opposition by filling jails, ordering executions, and exiling opposers of his regime.

3. In Eastern Europe, the USSR violently crushed rebellions against Soviet control in East Germany, Hungary, and Czechoslovakia in the three decades after World War II.

D. VIOLENCE AS A WAY TO PROMOTE CHANGE

1. Extremist organizations like Al-Qaeda used terrorism to promote their radical Islamic agenda, most infamously on September 11, 2001, in the U.S.

VIII. END OF THE COLD WAR

A. SIGNS OF STRAIN APPEARED IN THE SOVIET ECONOMY IN THE 1970s

The USSR's military rivaled that of the U.S., but at home, consumer goods were either hard to find or of poor quality. The Soviet Union was mired in a costly war in Afghanistan. After 1980, U.S. President Ronald Reagan increased military spending, gambling that the Soviets would choose to do the same and ignore calls for improved goods and services at home. They did.

B. IN THE MID-1980s THE REFORMER MIKHAIL GORBACHEV WAS BROUGHT TO POWER IN THE USSR

Gorbachev proposed introducing limited capitalism and loosening restrictions on criticism of the government. He thought these measures, if doled out in a controlled fashion, would restore the crumbling economy and people's faith in the communist system. It did neither. The world was amazed as former Soviet-controlled nations in Eastern Europe peacefully broke with communism in the late 1980s with nary a peep from Gorbachev.

C. In 1991, Gorbachev announced the break-up of the USSR. Russia became—on paper at least—a capitalist-based democracy, but over time, authoritarianism regained a foothold under the leadership of Vladimir Putin.

IX. CAUSATION IN THE AGE OF THE COLD WAR AND DECOLONIZATION

A. CONSEQUENCES OF THE COLD WAR

1. Cost. The Cold War involved expenditures of many billions of dollars on both sides of the conflict, especially by the main antagonists the U.S. and USSR. Proponents argue that the money spent was much less than what would have been appropriated if there had been a "hot" war between the rivals, not to mention the cost in human lives.

2. Nuclear legacy. The enormous destructive power of nuclear bombs may well have been the deciding factor as to why the Cold War did not turn "hot." The major rivals may have avoided using nuclear weapons, but after the Cold War, many nations developed or tried to build their own nuclear arsenal. Few responded positively to calls from the U.S., the former USSR, or the UN to curtail their nuclear programs. India, Pakistan, and Iran are some examples.

B. CAUSES OF DECOLONIZATION

The weakened state of colonial powers after two world wars gave the colonies an opportunity to break away, but other factors were involved:

1. A major purpose of the UN was to promote self-determination for peoples. By the end of the 20th century, almost every colony that wanted to, had attained self-rule.

2. Strong nationalist feelings in the colonies promoted a sense of destiny among leaders of independence movements. For example, the peoples in Indo-China drew on their national identities to outlast French and U.S. efforts to maintain the status quo.

Test Tip

To help prepare you to respond to questions about the Cold War era, rank five significant effects of the Cold War. Cite specific examples to defend your choices.

Next, answer this prompt: To what extent can the independence movements be called successful by the end of the 20th century? Defend your response with specific examples.

UNIT 9

Globalization
c. 1900 to the Present

After the Cold War, when communism in Eastern Europe fell and began to weaken in other regions, an American economist claimed we were at "the end of history." Part of what he meant was, the world of "bi-polarism" in which two superpowers competed for global domination, was over. Since then, much has been written about the "ever shrinking world" and the "rising global community." But, as with everything in history, those arguments are not entirely true.

I. ADVANCES IN TECHNOLOGY AND EXCHANGE AFTER 1900

The 20th century saw technological advances in greater numbers and with more frequency than ever before. Societies often struggled to adapt to the rapid changes.

A. COMMUNICATION

1. The telephone was invented in 1876 in the U.S. Until the 1920s in the West, it was known as an electrical toy used mainly by the rich and privileged in the "developed" countries of Europe, Australia, North and South America, and Japan. In the economic boom of the "Roaring Twenties" that occurred in most Western nations, more people could afford to have a telephone in their homes. That technology remained almost unchanged until the 1980s, when cell phones became available in large cities. The pattern repeated itself early on as only the wealthy could afford cell phones, but as prices went down, popularity went up. By the early 21st century, cell phones had become almost a necessity in the industrialized, developed world.

2. Radio/TV: Originally considered a device for one-to-one communication—a "wireless telegraph"—by the 1920s, radio

networks began broadcasting entertainment and news to national audiences. Television gained popularity after World War II, so much so that by the 1960s in the U.S., more homes had TVs than indoor toilets. It rapidly became more popular than radio as a source of information and entertainment. Both radio and television were used by governments to propagate their messages to citizens and foes alike.

3. Internet: Originally designed as a way for scientists to communicate computer data across telephone lines in the 1960s, the internet became a global phenomenon by the mid-1990s. Electronic mail (email) developed into a must-have instant communication service. By 2000, the internet connected billions of people and businesses, but there were still many areas with little or no internet access, primarily in rural Africa and Central Asia.

B. TRANSPORTATION

1. Automobiles

   i. Motorized vehicles were introduced in Germany in the late 19th century, but like radios and telephones, they did not become popular in the industrialized world until the 1920s. When automobiles did become popular, they changed many aspects of Western society. One big change was that people became more mobile. They were less likely to live their entire lives in one place. Residing in the "suburbs" and working miles away in city centers became popular. Driving to distant vacation spots—in Europe, that could mean in another country—was also possible.

   ii. Cars also created new industries and jobs: multinational corporations that sold petroleum products, the travel industry, and government-funded modern road construction, to name a few. The automobile's popularity also meant less use of public transportation, crowded rush-hours, traffic deaths, and increased air pollution.

2. Airplanes

   i.   The first wide-scale use of airplanes was in World War II.

   ii. Air travel in the West was for the wealthy (and military pilots) until after World War II, when an unprecedented economic boom occurred and the middle class could afford to join "the jet set." By the end of the 20th century, passenger air travel was commonplace in the West, but did not surpass the use of the automobile.

   iii. One casualty of air travel in many Western nations was the passenger train, which had been the most popular form of mass travel for almost 100 years.

3. Space Travel

   i.   Although not a common way of traveling, its introduction in the mid-20th century heralded a technological step that humans had dreamed about for millennia.

   ii. Liquid-fueled rockets were experimental in the 1920s and used as weapons by Germany in World War II. The Soviet Union launched the first missile to orbit the Earth in the 1950s, followed quickly by their rival, the U.S.

   iii. Western nations feared nuclear bombs would be launched from space. A "race to the Moon" fired Cold War imaginations in the 1960s and was won by the U.S. After the fall of communism in Russia in the early 1990s, the U.S. and Russia became partners in space exploration with a jointly-run International Space Station. By the early 21st century, other nations had launched missiles into space, particularly China and the European Space Agency.

C. ENERGY

1. Fossil fuels. Coal was an energy source around the world for many centuries, but the Industrial Revolution's powerful machines demanded unprecedented amounts of fuel. Diesel and gasoline, refined from petroleum ("rock oil") in the second half of the 19th century, was an even more efficient fuel supply, and industrial production increased even more. Like coal, processing petroleum products can damage the environment. Throughout the 20th century, governments and fuel-related businesses struggled to find a balance between society's

demands for these fuels and the health of the environment. By the end of this era, despite some implementation of other forms of energy such as solar and wind power, fossil fuels remained the cheapest and most-utilized source of energy.

2. Nuclear energy. This struggle was particularly intense over the use of atomic energy power plants. In the 1950s in the Western nations and in the USSR, atomic energy was promoted as the clean, efficient energy source of the future, but over time it lost favor. In 1979, a nuclear plant in the U.S. narrowly avoided a nuclear disaster and in 1986 in the USSR, the Chernobyl nuclear facility exploded, creating unprecedented destruction from a non-military atomic source.

3. Electric power. Beginning in the late 1800s, in cities in the U.S. and Western Europe, electric power arrived in homes and businesses. As the 20th century progressed, more and more people were added to the electrical grid. Electric lights, stoves, refrigerators, and radios were among the first electric appliances that people came to take for granted in the West. Electricity in homes and businesses changed people's sleep, work patterns, and consumer choices. By the end of the century, most of the populated world had access to electricity, but significant areas—especially in Africa—remained without lights.

D. BIRTH CONTROL

1. Better medicine, more plentiful food, and healthier habits meant persons in the 20th century lived longer than ever before. Longer life tends to mean more births. Population growth increased dramatically in the 20th century, but there were signs of slowing globally by the early 2000s (see chart on the following page). The greatest number of people were concentrated in South and East Asia, which has been the norm for recorded history.

2. In many cultures, artificial birth control was taboo. In 1960, the contraceptive "Pill" was developed and rapidly became popular with women with access to it. This convenient birth control method and the rise of women's rights led to a "sexual revolution" in the 1960s, starting in the West.

3. Concerns over high population rates led some nations— China and India in particular—to initiate government policies to limit the number of births. For example, China enacted

a "One Child Policy" aimed at urban couples. By the year 2000, its population was over one billion. India adopted a National Population Policy to curb birthrates, but its population continued to climb.

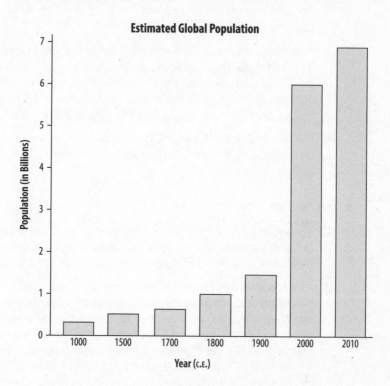

Estimated Global Population

The AP® World History: Modern exam favors questions about global population numbers, especially after the discovery of the Americas by Europeans and the Industrial Revolution.

E. GREEN REVOLUTION

1. In the mid-20th century, the development of powerful fertilizers and pesticides combined with new high-yield, disease-resistant crops led to predictions of a famine-free world. Proposed by the U.S. after World War II and promoted by the UN, the "Green Revolution" held out hope that food could be grown almost everywhere. Although food production skyrocketed through the Green Revolution, so did the global population.

2. India was an early participant in the Green Revolution in the 1960s. New hybrid rice crops grown in combination with strong pesticides produced very high yields—so much so that India seemed to end its long cycle of periodic famine and became a leader in rice exports. Corn and wheat were other popular hybrid crops.

3. Attempts to spread the Green Revolution yielded mixed results: in the Philippines, rice yields soared, but in much of Africa agricultural production stagnated. Shifting weather patterns contributed to Africa's lower crop yield as have the destructive nature of many civil wars since the end of World War II.

4. Despite setbacks, the world food supply increased tremendously because of the Green Revolution—but so had global population.

F. MEDICINE

1. Throughout history, infant mortality has been the greatest factor in limiting life expectancy. Children who survived past their fifth birthday could generally expect to live into their 60s.

2. As a result of systematic scientific research from universities, hospitals, and medical-related corporations, medicines, healthier lifestyles, and surgical techniques greatly increased life expectancy. The polio vaccine, antibiotics, improved surgical procedures like sterilizing equipment, and advances in cancer treatments all contributed. Deadly infectious diseases such as smallpox and whooping cough were virtually eliminated through global campaigns of inoculation.

3. Medical advances, however, were largely limited to industrialized nations. In 2011, for example, 26 nations with the lowest life expectancy were in Africa.

4. An unexpected outcome of longer life was the increase in frequency later in life of heart disease and Alzheimer's disease.

G. SCIENCE AND SOCIETY

1. From advances in scientific knowledge since the Scientific Revolution in the 17th century, people's great faith in science in the West affected society itself. For example, after Darwin published his Theory of Evolution in the 19th century, debates arose in the West over religious faith and scientific reason,

which continued past the 20th century. Other scientific pronouncements also made a significant mark on societies.

2. In the early 20th century, the German physicist Albert Einstein developed the theory of relativity that overturned long-held ideas about a constant, clock-like universe. It proposed instead that space and time can vary, depending on the point of view of the observer. In this new view of the universe and humanity's place in it, there are no absolutes.

3. This take on the universe had a tremendous impact on Western society after the unexpected massive destruction of World War I. To many, the view of an ordered, rational universe no longer made sense. Philosophers, artists, composers, and theologians took the scientific concept of relativity and applied it to society. Right and wrong were no longer absolutes, but instead were concepts for each individual to determine. For example, abstract artists wanted the viewer to decide what a painting "says." The expression, "It's all relative," has its roots in Einstein's 1905 theory of relativity.

II. TECHNOLOGICAL ADVANCES AND LIMITATIONS AFTER 1900: DISEASE

A. PANDEMICS

1. The first truly global disease epidemic was the 1918 influenza pandemic that killed roughly 20 million people. It is thought that soldiers returning from World War I carried the disease to their home countries. Throughout the 20th century, new flu outbreaks continued, but were not as deadly.

2. HIV/AIDS was the second major modern pandemic—as many as 25 million stricken people died by the early 21st century. First identified in the late 20th century, HIV spread in the West through sexual contact and by illicit drug-needle sharing. It then entered undetected into hospital blood supplies and was transmitted via transfusions. Governments worked with private pharmaceutical companies to develop vaccines against the disease.

3. AIDS remains a leading cause of death in Africa, accounting for 2 million of the 2.8 million people who died worldwide in 2007. Government programs promoting both abstinence and

"safe sex" had slowed the effects of AIDS on that continent by the early 21st century.

4. On regional levels, malaria, tuberculosis, and cholera were eliminated in the industrialized world but continued to kill people in lesser developed areas.

B. FAMINE

1. One result of modern war on civilians is the disruption of the food supply. Famine struck Europe after World War I. Most of the 20 million deaths in the Russian civil war were attributed to famine.

2. Government policies of denying food to those deemed an enemy of the state killed many millions. In the 1930s, Stalin enacted an "artificial famine" against rural communities that resisted his rule in the USSR and millions died. Recall that in the mid-20th century, Mao's insistence during the "Great Leap Forward" to favor industrial development over agricultural production caused perhaps 20 million deaths in China.

3. Natural disasters such as droughts and floods in China, India, and East Africa killed millions more from 1900 onward. High population densities in East and South Asia heightened death tolls from such events, despite international relief campaigns.

 ## III. TECHNOLOGICAL ADVANCES: DEBATES ABOUT THE ENVIRONMENT AFTER 1900

"Environment" in terms of AP® World History: Modern means more than just trees, birds, and rivers. People, and how they interact with their environment, are also integral pieces of the puzzle. More people make more demands for more crops and require more land to live on and more housing for shelter. This affects the environment.

A. Criticisms of the Green Revolution included environmental concerns against overuse of pesticides and fertilizers; the tendency of farmers to plant "monocrops" instead of a variety of grains as they once had; and unprecedented population growth. More food means more people can eat, and thus live and reproduce. But from a long-term global perspective, experts wonder whether the

Green Revolution can continue to feed ever-increasing numbers of people.

B. POLLUTION AND DEFORESTATION

Along with the benefits of enormous industrial growth came pollution of the environment on levels unseen before. Pollution like waste-water or smoke from fires has always been a part of society, but mass production of goods often meant mass production of waste products that were dispersed into surrounding rivers, the ground, and the air. (You read about some effects of pollution in 19th century Britain in Chapter 8.)

1. Deforestation, the cutting down of trees on a large scale with no plan to replant them, became a growing concern after World War II. Deforestation is driven by the need to make room to plant crops or to harvest desirable types of wood such as mahogany for global markets. Areas most affected are the disappearing rainforests.

2. In 1970, a grassroots pro-environment event—Earth Day—led to more government regulation of industrial pollution in the capitalist West. After the fall of communism in Eastern Europe, massive industrial pollution was uncovered unlike anything seen in the West.

 IV. ECONOMICS IN THE GLOBAL AGE

A. LATE 20th-CENTURY ECONOMIC CHANGES

1. After World War II, several organizations promoted capitalism through international trade and financial assistance to poorer nations and regions. The World Bank and the International Monetary Fund (IMF) promoted sound banking principles and loaned money to nations with developing economies. GATT, or the General Agreement on Tariffs and Trade, promoted international free trade. The World Trade Organization (WTO) replaced it in the late 20th century.

2. The G7, founded in the 1970s, was an organization representing the interests of the world's seven largest economies. It has since expanded to the G20. The communist version was Comecon, founded by the USSR. It disbanded after the fall of communism in Russia and Eastern Europe at the end of the 20th century.

3. During the 1980s, a trend toward more capitalist economic policies swept the globe. Tax cuts and less government intervention in business practices were championed by U.S. President Ronald Reagan and British Prime Minister Margaret Thatcher. Many Latin American nations followed suit, not only enacting similar economic reforms, but also increasing pro-democracy policies.

4. After Mao's death, Deng Xiaoping ended the Cultural Revolution and boosted China's economy by inviting government-monitored capitalist investment from the West. The economy and people's standard of living boomed into the early 21st century, but political reforms didn't follow.

5. Not all political and economic movements meant democratic rule and capitalism after the Cold War. Dictatorships and kingdoms remained in many Middle Eastern nations. In China, a pro-democracy movement led by students in 1989 was brutally crushed in Beijing's Tiananmen Square, even as the communist regime there was allowing more capitalism.

6. In the 1960s and beyond, the "Asian Tigers" of Singapore, Hong Kong, South Korea, and Taiwan experienced enormous economic growth, centered on banking and exports. By the end of the 20th century, Indonesia and Vietnam were emerging Southeast Asian economies.

Test Tip

The writers of the AP® World History exam are fond of questions about globalism after World War II.

B. REGIONAL TRADE AGREEMENTS ALSO DEVELOPED

1. The European Union. The EU had its genesis in the 1950s when six Western European nations lowered trade barriers between themselves to help compete against the giant U.S. economy. The group had several names until the early 1990s, when it was called the European Union. Most of the first twelve member nations in Western Europe adopted a single monetary unit, the Euro. (Britain declined.)

2. After the fall of communism in Eastern Europe, the EU invited other nations to join. By the early 21st century, 27 nations comprised the EU. In its various forms, the EU oversaw a

booming economy in the 1950s and 1960s, a major recession in the 1970s, and mild economic growth from the 1980s to the present.

3. In response to the success of the European Union, the U.S., Mexico, and Canada entered into a free trade agreement called NAFTA in the early 1990s. But it did not include the political aspects of the EU's organization.

4. In 1960, oil-rich nations, primarily from the Middle East, but also from Africa and South America, organized a cartel, that sought to set the global price of crude oil. The Organization of Petroleum Exporting Countries (OPEC) became a household word in the West when it raised prices and reduced its exports of oil to Western Europe and the U.S. after the 1973 Arab-Israeli War.

5. Throughout the 1970s, the double-whammy of higher oil prices and reduced supplies damaged Western economies. Inflation soared and unemployment rose. As a result, the West and the Arab world realized how dependent the West was on imported petroleum.

C. TRANSNATIONAL (MULTINATIONAL) CORPORATIONS

In a trend that started in the 19th century, corporations that "went global" boomed after World War II. Exxon, McDonald's, General Motors, and Coca-Cola were based in the U.S., but expanded to markets around the globe. Philips Electronics and Shell Oil Corporation based their international operations with headquarters in Europe. From East Asia, Sony Electronics, Toyota Motors, and Hyundai Motors shipped products around the world. Online commerce became a multi-billion-dollar enterprise beginning in the late 1990s through companies like eBay and Alibaba.

V. CALLS FOR REFORM AND RESPONSES AFTER 1900

A. UNIVERSAL DECLARATION OF HUMAN RIGHTS

In 1948, the UN echoed the concepts from the Nuremberg Trials with its Universal Declaration of Human Rights. Among them are: freedom of speech and religion; the right to life, liberty, and personal security; freedom of movement from another country or within a country; and the right to a fair trial, work, and education. While all member UN nations signed the Declaration, not all fully participated in exercising the rights enshrined in it.

B. WOMEN'S RIGHTS

In the early 20th century, adult women in some Western nations received the right to vote, but other inequalities in society remained. As part of the civil rights movements that swept the West beginning in the 1950s, women's groups in the U.S., Europe, and Japan actively sought equal employment opportunities, as well as educational, political, and social equality with men. The UN proclaimed 1975, "International Women's Year," to promote women's rights.

1. However, despite civil rights gains made in Western cultures and increased governmental participation by women in communist nations such as China and the USSR during the 20th century, in many areas of the world, human rights violations remained into the 21st century. Children were forced into armies in Sudan, ethnic genocide killed almost a million people in and around Rwanda, and women were refused educational opportunities by the Taliban in Afghanistan—to list just a few examples.

C. CHANGES IN BELIEF SYSTEMS

In the early 1960s, Pope John XXIII called for revisions to the centuries-old traditions in the Roman Catholic Church. More participation by non-clergy in church services was encouraged and the Mass was no longer conducted in Latin, but in the language of the local church. Pope John and his successors, most notably John Paul II, also promoted ecumenism—cooperation between faiths.

1. Asian religions gained followers in the West, particularly Buddhism. Part of the reason may have been the ecumenical spirit begun in the 1960s and another, the global popularity of the Beatles, who introduced aspects of South Asian music and faith to the West.

2. Some branches of Islam went through a conservative revival. Beginning in the 1950s, partly as a response against the growing influence of Western culture that came from contacts made in the oil trade, Islamic fundamentalism rejected the "decadent" culture of the West. Islamic fundamentalism's most

famous examples were found in the Iranian Revolution in the 1970s and in the formation of terrorist groups such as Al-Qaeda (see Chapter 11).

3. The legal caste system was officially banned in India in the 1950s, but society was slow to fully embrace that reform.

 VI. GLOBALIZED CULTURE AFTER 1900

A. POPULAR CULTURE AND GLOBAL CONSUMERISM

After World War II, the West dominated the world's economy and had the most multinational corporations. The U.S. produced half of the world's goods for most of the post-World War II era and had the means, through its global corporations, to distribute them around the world. The advent of global television in the 1960s, due to communications satellites, increased the connectedness of the world.

1. Cultural examples include American clothing styles, music (like Elvis Presley or "The Twist" dance craze), movies, and television shows. Others include the British rock group The Beatles, whose popularity around the world eclipsed even Elvis. Bollywood, the nickname for India's film industry, produced more films than Hollywood by the end of the 20th century, and became popular in the West.

2. K-Pop from South Korea and anime from Japan became a global phenomenon after the rise of the internet.

3. International popularity of sports followed the spread of TV and the internet. The Olympics and World Cup soccer became must-see global events. American sports, such as baseball and basketball, had many participants and fans in Europe and Asia, so much so that by the end of the decade European and Asian professional athletes were playing for teams in the U.S.

4. Social media like Facebook and Twitter connected billions worldwide through the internet.

Expect questions on the AP® exam about the spread of popular culture after World War II.

VII. RESISTANCE TO GLOBALIZATION AFTER 1900

Some individuals and groups saw the rise of free markets as only benefiting the already-wealthy economies at the expense of less-developed ones. Groups such as Antifa and the Peoples' Global Action protested in cities holding meetings of groups like the G20 and the WTO (pg. 129).

The following discussion of 19th-century institutions is a good example of using the historical skill of context.

VIII. INSTITUTIONS DEVELOPING IN A GLOBALIZED WORLD

A. 19th-CENTURY PREDECESSORS TO LATER INSTITUTIONS

1. Institutions promoting international cooperation date to the mid-19th century with the Red Cross founded in Britain. It is a private organization, but works with government agencies around the world. Amnesty International raises awareness of the plight of political prisoners everywhere.

2. The Universal Postal Union and the International Telecommunication Union founded in the late 19th century are still in operation. Their job is to create agreements between member nations regarding exchanging international mail and communications, such as telephone, radio, and internet usage.

3. Rapid train transportation and the development of long-distance telegraph communication led to international agreements establishing the world's time zones.

4. The International Olympic Committee was also formed in the late 19th century. Its purpose was to promote international understanding through sport. The Olympics grew in popularity as the 20th century progressed.

B. 20th CENTURY GLOBAL INSTITUTIONS

1. The League of Nations (see Chapter 10) disbanded and was replaced after World War II by the UN.

2. The UN had more power than the League of Nations. Most importantly, unlike the League, the UN set up a Security Council which can use military force to battle aggressive member countries. The UN sent soldiers into combat in the Korean War in the 1950s and in the Persian Gulf War in the 1990s.

3. The World Health Organization is a UN agency that combats infectious diseases and promotes the general health of all citizens. UNICEF, another UN agency, works for children's rights, and their development and protection around the globe.

IX. CONTINUITY AND CHANGE IN A GLOBALIZED WORLD

So much change in the 20th century! And yet, continuities persisted. For an exercise in the skill of argumentation, rank six of the greatest changes in the 20th century. Pick one from each of the six AP® history themes: politics/governments, societies, economics, cultures, technologies, and/or the environment. Defend your first and last choices using specific examples in your arguments.

Next, rank any four continuities across the 20th century from most important to least and defend each choice with specific examples in your arguments.

PART III

REVIEW CHARTS

Art, Architecture, and Literature Review

The chapters in Part II: Chronological Review cite several important references to literature, government documents, art, and architecture. Below is a handy table with important trends in art and architecture and essential examples of literature in world history since c. 1200.

UNITS 1 AND 2 | c. 1200 to c. 1450

ART	ARCHITECTURE	LITERATURE/ DOCUMENTS
Christian iconography—Europe and Byzantine	Gothic cathedrals— Europe Hagia Sofia—Byzantine church (Turkey) Rock churches— Ethiopia	Journals from Marco Polo (Italy) and Ibn Battuta (North Africa)
Islamic art on life of Muhammad—North Africa to South Asia	Mosques, minarets, courtyard complexes— North Africa to South Asia Great Zimbabwe complex—Southeast Africa	"Arabic" numerals, calligraphy, Muslim science journals, Ibn Khaldun's histories, *1001 Nights*— Southwest Asia, North Africa
Song Dynasty ceramics	Mississippian mounds—(southeast U.S.) Aztec Templo Mayor— Mesoamerica Inca ; Machu Picchu— Peru	Block printing—China Movable-type printing—Korea

UNITS 3 AND 4 | c. 1450 to c. 1750

ART	ARCHITECTURE	LITERATURE/ DOCUMENTS
Renaissance Revival of Greco/Roman art styles—Europe	European influences in Latin American buildings	Moveable type printing press; Copernicus's heliocentric theory published—Europe
Mughal court paintings	European palaces: Versailles (France) and the Hermitage (Russia)	Martin Luther's *95 Theses,* Treaty of Tordesillas, writings by Shakespeare, *Two Treatises on Government* and other writings of the Enlightenment—Europe
Qing Dynasty imperial portraits	Mughal buildings such as the Taj Mahal—India	Block printing—Japan
Aztec and Inca paintings that depict the Spanish conquest	Ottoman repurposing of Hagia Sophia	Edicts of Tokugawa Shogunate Closing Japan

UNITS 5 AND 6 | c. 1750 to c. 1900

ART	ARCHITECTURE	LITERATURE/ DOCUMENTS
Romanticism (ex. by David) Realism (ex. Courbet) Impressionism (ex. Van Gogh)—Europe	Neoclassicism— Europe Brick and steel skyscrapers—Europe, the U.S.	*Declaration of Independence*—U.S. *Declaration of the Rights of Man and the Citizen*—France *Jamaica Letter*—Latin America
Japanese and Chinese depictions of Westerners and Western Technology	Western-influenced building styles—South, East, and Southeast Asia, Africa	*Letter to Queen Victoria*—China *Treaty of Nanjing*— China *Communist Manifesto* and *On the Origin of Species*—Britain
Ukiyo-e prints of landscapes and seascapes—Japan	Crystal Palace—Britain	*Tanzimat constitution*— Ottoman Empire *Meiji constitution*— Japan *What Is to Be Done?*; *Emancipation Manifesto*—Russia

UNITS 7, 8, AND 9 | 1900 to the present

ART	ARCHITECTURE	LITERATURE/ DOCUMENTS
Cubism, Abstract art, Dadaism—Europe, the U.S. *Guernica*—Europe	Bauhaus style—Europe Glass and steel skyscrapers—Europe, the U.S., East Asia, Southeast Asia	*Treaty of Versailles*— League of Nations *Mein Kampf*—Germany *Three Principles of the People*—China
Propaganda posters for World Wars I and II—Global	Art Deco style— Western nations and their colonies	*Universal Declaration of Human Rights*—United Nations
Socialist Realism— USSR, China	Social housing architecture—Eastern- and Western-bloc nations	*Writings by Gandhi*— India *Writings by Martin Luther King, Jr.; The Feminine Mystique, Betty Friedan*—U.S.

Important Civilizations, Empires, and Dynasties

In each of the major chronological eras in AP® World History: Modern, some civilizations are featured more prominently than others. Following are the "all-stars" of each era, arranged by their geographic region of influence. World history before c. 1200 is included to assist you with historical context of post-1200 societies. As you study, note the civilizations that cut across multiple time periods and/or geographic regions.

CIVILIZATIONS OF INFLUENCE IN SPECIFIC TIME PERIODS

Geographic Region	to c. 600 BCE	c. 600 BCE to c. 600 CE	c. 600 CE to c. 1450 CE
Southwest Asia	Mesopotamia, Persia	Hellenism, Parthian	Abbasid, Ottoman, Mongols
West Africa			Ghana
East Africa	Bantus	Bantus	Ethiopia, Zimbabwe, Swahili States
North Africa	Egypt, Kush	Hellenism	Arab, Ottoman
Mediterranean		Greek, Roman ("Mediterranean Civilization")	Byzantine
South Asia	Indus Valley	Mauryan, Gupta	Delhi Sultanates
East Asia	Shang	Qin, Han	Tang, Song, Mongol (Yuan), Ming
Central Asia	Persian	Mongols	
Americas	Olmec, Chavin	Mayan, Teotihuacan, Moche	Maya, Aztec
Europe			Muslim Iberia (Portugal and Spain)

(continued)

Geographic Region	c. 1450 to c. 1750	c. 1750 to c. 1900	c. 1900 to the present
Southwest Asia	Ottoman, Safavid	Ottoman	Ottoman, Britain, France, Israel, Iran, Iraq, Saudi Arabia, Turkey
West Africa	Songhay	Influence from Western Europe	
East Africa	Ethiopia	Influence from Western Europe	Influence from Western Europe
North Africa	Arab, Ottoman	Influence from Western Europe	Algeria, Egypt
Mediterranean	Ottoman	Ottoman	
South Asia	Mughal	British Raj	India, Pakistan
East Asia	Ming, Qing (Manchu), Tokugawa Shogunate	Qing (Manchu), Meiji, European "spheres of influence"	China, Japan, Korea, "Asian Tigers"
Central Asia	Mughals		
Americas	Aztec, Inca, influence from Western Europe	U.S., Mexico, Haiti, Brazil	U.S., Mexico, Cuba, Panama
Europe	Portugal, Spain, France, Britain, Holland, Holy Roman Empire, Russia	Western Europe, Russia	Axis Powers, Allies, North Atlantic Treaty Organization (NATO), Warsaw Pact, European Union

Important Migration and Trade Routes

On the AP® World History: Modern exam, it is important to know the movement of people (migration) and trade networks over time. Study the outline below of a few examples of migration and trade patterns, and make connections to what you learned in the chapters in Part II about the political, social, and economic causes and effects of migration and of trade. Eras before c. 1200 are included to provide you with historical context of migration and trade patterns.

I. MIGRATIONS

A. c. 600 BCE–c. 600 CE

1. Central Asia into Europe (Huns)

2. Germanic peoples within Europe (e.g., Goths and Vandals)

3. Continued Bantu migration

B. c. 600–c. 1450

1. Turkic migrations from central Asia to Southwest Asia

2. Vikings from northern Europe into France, Russia, Iceland, and Greenland

3. Mongols south and west across Asia and into eastern Europe

4. Arabs across North Africa and into Spain

C. c. 1450–c. 1750

1. Europeans to the Americas

2. Africans into Southwest Asia, Europe, and the Americas

D. c. 1750–c. 1900

1. Europeans to the Americas

2. South Asians and East Asians to the Americas, Africa, Southeast Asia, and Oceania

E. c. 1900 to the present

1. South and Central Americans to North America

2. Migrations between India and Pakistan after the Partition

3. Africans into Europe

4. South Asians into the Middle East, North America, and Europe

5. Former colonial subjects from Africa and Asia to cities in Europe

II. TRADE AREAS AND TERMS

The AP® World History: Modern exam assesses your grasp of trade regions and what was exchanged in those regions over time. Study the merchandise, religions, diseases, and technologies in the outline below. Important terms are included below each time frame.

A. c. 1200–c. 1450

➤ **Important trade regions:**

- Silk Roads
- Indian Ocean
- South China Sea
- Mediterranean
- Trans-Sahara
- Black Sea
- Mesoamerica
- Andes

➤ **Terms involving trade:** caravanserai, *dhows*, *junks*, decline and revival of trade cities, lateen sails, monsoon winds, oasis, camels, Ibn Battuta, Marco Polo, Pax Mongolica, Black Death/Bubonic Plague, Straits of Malacca, Srivijaya Empire, Inca roads, Islamic merchants, Dar al-Islam, Mansa Musa, Zheng He, porcelain from China

B. c. 1450–c. 1750

➤ **Important trade areas:**

- Atlantic World

- Indian Ocean

- South China Sea

- Russia

➤ **Terms:** Columbian Exchange, global trade network, African slave trade, mercantilism, joint-stock companies, Potosi (South America), British raj, Russian fur trade, silver.

C. c. 1750–c. 1900

➤ **Important trade areas:**

- Europe to its colonies in Africa and Asia

- Atlantic World

- Russia

- Suez Canal

➤ **Terms:** industrialization, imperialism, capitalism, Marxism, trade unions, steamships, trains, Opium Wars, spheres of influence, Meiji Restoration, open-door policy, transnational businesses.

Review Charts

D. c. 1900 to the present

➤ **Important trade areas:**

- Panama Canal
- Pacific Rim
- Persian Gulf
- the internet

➤ **Terms:** Great Depression, New Deal, fascism, communism, OPEC, U.S. economic power, "coca-colonialism," European Union, NAFTA, free trade, World Bank, World Trade Organization, multinational/transnational corporations, Asian Tigers, online commerce.

Important Technology

"When did people start using *that*?" It depends on where the people were at the time. You know from your studies that *technology*—making and using tools to change the natural state of the environment—isn't an instant global event. The list below highlights major technological developments and the first known places they occurred. Some came along at later times, independently, and in different regions. Many ideas spread along trade routes from their places of origin. As you review this list after studying the historical review in Part II, consider the effects these inventions had on societies.

c. 1200–c. 1450

➤ Paper money, block printing, Ming "treasure ships," firearms: China

➤ Mechanical clock, eyeglasses, wheeled plow: Europe

➤ Lateen sail, astrolabe, university system of education: across Dar al-Islam

➤ Chinampas (floating gardens): Central Mexico

➤ Inca road and bridge systems: South America

c. 1450–c. 1750

➤ Movable-type printing press; map of world; telescope; caravel, microscope; steam engine; factory textile machines: Europe

c. 1750–c. 1900

➤ Steamboat, steam locomotive, telegraph, steel ships, steel-framed skyscrapers, machine gun, light bulb, telephone, radio, typewriter, movie projector, electric and gasoline motors, cotton gin, sewing machine, textile factories steel plow, mechanical reaper, automobile: Europe and the U.S.

c. 1900 TO THE PRESENT

➤ Airplane, liquid-fuel rocket, communications satellite, nuclear power, television, transistor, electronic computer, the internet, penicillin, Green Revolution, birth control ("the Pill"), electronic medical imaging: the U.S. and Europe

PART IV

TEST-TAKING STRATEGIES AND PRACTICE QUESTIONS

Strategies for the Multiple-Choice Questions

The AP® World History: Modern exam begins with a 55-question, 55-minute multiple-choice section that is worth 40% of your total grade. Although the AP® World History: Modern Course and Exam Description says that the course runs "to the present," the reality is that the exam creators know that most teachers won't get much past the end of the Cold War in the early 1990s. So the test writers tend not to ask many questions beyond that date. So be sure to do a quick review of the highlights of the post–Cold War era if your class didn't get there by early May.

In addition, looking at the early chapters of this book, you'll see that the exam questions are divided into four time frames: c. 1200–c. 1450, c. 1450–c. 1750, c. 1750–c. 1900, and c. 1900 to the present. The era c. 1200–c. 1450 is worth 16% to 20% of the exam. Each of the other eras accounts for 24% to 30% of the exam. So, there should be around ten multiple-choice questions from 1200–1450. Remember: that era also includes the background material about the origins of major belief systems. Each of the later three units should have thirteen to seventeen multiple-choice questions. In other words, there are no eras you can take lightly, and it also means the last 100+ years are as important as the 300 years from 1450 to 1750.

Some multiple-choice questions are comparative. That is, you are asked to compare societies in different time periods. It's important to understand that the AP® World History: Modern exam is all about comparisons across time and place—getting the big picture and making connections. Many multiple-choice questions will involve only one time period. Some multiple-choice questions will feel like "gimmes," while others will be brain-rattling hard. That's to be expected. Hardly anyone ever gets all the multiple-choice questions right, so even if you miss 15 or 20, you're still doing better than most.

What you *won't* find on the AP® World History: Modern exam are "recall" multiple-choice questions. Here's an example:

The Tang Empire was in

(A) China

(B) Mesoamerica

(C) India

(D) Europe

By the way, the answer is choice (A). Instead, what you will find are sets of 3 to 4 questions that are anchored to some type of stimulus, such as a document, chart, map, or art. Some of the multiple-choice questions will be more directly connected to the stimulus than others. Look below for some examples.

To answer 55 questions in 55 minutes means you get 60 seconds to answer each question. Math is so easy! That might not sound like a lot of time, but with practice, you'll find that it is. Study the stimulus first, so you know generally what the answer choices that follow will cover.

The best way to deal with fears of running out of time is to first answer all the multiple-choice questions that seem easy to you. When you get to the end of the multiple-choice section, go back and spend time on the ones you didn't answer during the first run-through. When the exam proctor calls "Time!," that's it. You can't return later and finish the multiple-choice section.

Test Tip

Keep in mind, especially if you or your teacher use multiple-choice questions from previous exams or older exam study guides for practice, that the exam begins c. 1200 and questions will be in sets linked to a document or image.

The multiple-choice questions should generally run in chronological order. That means the first questions should come from the earliest time periods and continue chronologically "to the present."

Answer all of the questions. Don't skip even one. If you have no idea, guess. Even if you have 10 questions to go and 30 seconds left, bubble in those ovals on the answer sheet. You have a 25% chance of getting each guess right, and that's a lot better than skipping a question and having a 0% chance.

Don't be discouraged if you "feel" like you missed too many multiple-choice questions. You can get about 20 of them wrong and still be in the "3" range headed into your short-answer and essay questions.

Practice Multiple-Choice Questions

Practice with the following AP®-style questions. Then go online to access our timed, full-length practice exam at *www.rea.com/studycenter*.

Use the excerpt below and your knowledge of world history to answer questions 1–3.

The Mongols persisted in their goal of conquering the whole world as if they were one man but they are millions in number. They attack suddenly, and make such horrible slaughters that the king cannot find enough people to wage battle against them. They fight constantly with javelins, bows and arrows, battle axes, maces, and swords. They trick all people and princes in time of peace, pretending to want to help but really to learn weaknesses and to find enough fertile ground to feed their huge multitudes. In this way they have deceived foolish rulers who granted the Mongols passage through their territories, which resulted in the ruin and destruction of the rulers and their lands.

From a 16th century English translation
of a 13th century Russian description
of Mongol characteristics

1. Modern historians would most likely consider this description of the Mongols to be

   (A) accurate because the translation was written during the era of Mongol conquests

   (B) balanced because the original author considered the Mongol point of view based on primary documents

   (C) questionable because the original author was from Russia, a region conquered by Mongols

   (D) inaccurate because the Mongol written language was not translated by Western scholars until the 20th century

2. The Mongol empire compared to other empires in history in what way?

   (A) It was the largest land empire of all time.

   (B) It was about the size of the Holy Roman Empire.

   (C) It lasted almost as long as the Ottoman Empire.

   (D) It used its naval military forces to create a Pacific Ocean empire.

3. According to most modern historians, in which of the following ways were the Mongols indirectly responsible for the spread of the pandemic plague in the 14th century?

   (A) Mongols released plague-infected rats into cities to weaken them.

   (B) Mongol intermarriage with local conquered people led to the spread of sexually transmitted diseases.

   (C) The decline of Mongol influence in the 14th century resulted in inadequate medical care in Eurasia.

   (D) Extensive trade routes protected by Mongols led to increased exchange of goods, technology, and disease.

Use the excerpt below and your knowledge
of world history to answer questions 4–6.

We live in an age of Enlightenment. The motto of
the Enlightenment should be, "Have courage to use
your own understanding!" A prince should allow
his people complete freedom of religion, and if he
does, he should be praised by all. Rulers should also
favor freedom in the arts and sciences and allow
his subjects to create better ways to draw up laws.
Once men are free to think for themselves, they will
increasingly be able to act freely. Eventually, even
the principles of government will benefit by treating
people with dignity.

Immanuel Kant, German political philosopher,
late 18th century

4. Which of the following was **NOT** a result of Enlightenment
   thought as described by Kant?

   (A) The Reformation

   (B) The American and French revolutions

   (C) The development of constitutional governments

   (D) The rise of nationalism, beginning in Europe

5. Enlightenment reforms included the abolition movement,
   which is best described as a political and social
   campaign to

   (A) clean up pollution from the Industrial Revolution

   (B) expand women's rights, including the right to vote

   (C) end slavery, beginning in European colonies

   (D) reform prisons and mental institutions

6. The most direct result of Enlightenment philosophy in the 20th century was which of the following?

    (A) Globalization of culture in media, such as "Bollywood" movies

    (B) Decolonization movements, especially in Asia and Africa

    (C) The rise of fascism as a form of government

    (D) The rise of fundamentalism in some religions

Use the excerpt below and your knowledge of world history to answer questions 7–9.

Another of their good qualities is their habit of wearing clean white garments on Fridays. Even if a man has nothing but an old worn shirt, he washes it and cleans it, and wears it to the Friday service. Yet another is their zeal for learning the Quran by heart. They put their children in chains if they show any backwardness in memorizing it, and they are not set free until they have it by heart.

Among their bad qualities are the following. Women go into the sultan's presence naked and without coverings, and his daughters also go about naked. Then there is their custom of putting dust and ashes on their heads, as a mark of respect, and other grotesque ceremonies. Another disgusting practice among many of them is the eating of dogs.

Ibn Battuta, 14th century Muslim traveler commenting on his visit to West Africa

7. Ibn Battuta describes a culture that blends traditions from different belief systems. World historians call this and the similar blending of traditions which of the following?

    (A) Syncretism

    (B) Global migration

    (C) Nationalism

    (D) Theocracy

8. West Africa saw a blending of Islamic teachings with local traditional beliefs. Which of the following is the clearest example of another such religious blending?

   (A) Theravada Buddhism in India

   (B) Judaism in Southwest Asia

   (C) Catholicism in Latin America

   (D) Daoism in Eastern Europe

9. What factor best explains why a Muslim from Spain or the Ottoman Empire could travel to and move about freely in West Africa in the 14th century?

   (A) Under European imperialism, travelers were granted freedom of religion in Africa.

   (B) West African governments had official political alliances with Spain and the Ottoman Empire.

   (C) West African governments paid for large numbers of Muslim immigrants to populate their nations.

   (D) Muslims from those regions shared a common religious faith with most people in West Africa.

Use the following document to answer questions 10–13.

"The bourgeoisie, wherever it has got the upper hand, has put an end to all feudal, patriarchal, idyllic relations. . . . It has resolved personal worth into exchange value, and in place of the numberless indefeasible chartered freedoms, has set up that single, unconscionable freedom—Free Trade. In one word, for exploitation, veiled by religious and political illusions, it has substituted naked, shameless, direct, brutal exploitation....The bourgeoisie . . . has converted the physician, the lawyer, the priest, the poet, the man of science, into its paid wage laborers. . . . The bourgeoisie has torn away from the family its sentimental veil, and has reduced the family relation to a mere money relation."

Karl Marx, *The Communist Manifesto*, 1848

10. What major historical development most likely triggered Marx's comments in this document?

   (A) The development of feudalism in western Europe

   (B) The rise of mercantilism by some western European states

   (C) The expansion of the Industrial Revolution

   (D) The effects of Russia's communist revolution

11. What changes to society and culture occurred in areas where the development referred to in the document was most pronounced in the mid-19th century?

   (A) Birthrates had declined compared to the late 18th century

   (B) Poor families began moving to the countryside to escape overcrowded cities

   (C) Working conditions in factories significantly improved

   (D) Legal labor unions successfully lobbied governments for minimum wage laws

12. By the mid-20th century, Marx's ideas had led to which of these developments?

   (A) An increase in the number of government-funded social welfare programs in Western democracies

   (B) A rise in the number of communist states

   (C) The beginnings of a global Cold War

   (D) All of these are true

13. By the end of the 20th century, what was the apparent outcome of Marx's ideas?

   (A) They continued to strengthen as a global political and economic system

   (B) They were holding steady as a global political and economic system, with no expansion or loss

   (C) They were largely on the decline as a political and economic system

   (D) They had been discredited and completely disappeared as a political and economic system.

Use the document below to answer questions 14–16.

1. No Japanese ships are allowed to leave for foreign countries
2. Any Japanese person must be executed for secretly trying to leave the country. Europeans who enter Japan illegally face the death penalty.
4. Any place that practices Christianity must be thoroughly investigated.
7. Any Westerners who spread Christianity may be jailed, as was done in the past.
10. Samurai are not allowed to purchase any goods from foreign ships directly from Chinese merchants in Nagasaki.

> The *Sakoku Edict* of 1635, by Japan's Tokugawa Shogunate, addressed to officials in the city of Nagasaki

14. The laws above were written in response to which of these global processes?

   (A) The Industrial Revolution

   (B) The Columbian Exchange

   (C) Implementation of Social Darwinist theories

   (D) The "White Man's Burden"

15. The Sakoku Edict is a response to this 17th century European economic theory that encouraged rulers and merchants to develop colonies that provided raw materials for global markets:

    (A) Mercantilism

    (B) Capitalism

    (C) Socialism

    (D) Nationalism

16. In the mid-19th century, Western nations forced the Tokugawa Shogunate to end Japan's isolationism.

    What was the name of the process that transformed Japan's political, social and economic policies?

    (A) The Bakufu

    (B) The Greater East Asia Co-Prosperity Sphere

    (C) The Meiji Restoration

    (D) The Samurai

Use the image below and your knowledge
of world history to answer questions 17–19.

The Library of Congress

1885 newspaper cartoon by American Thomas Nast titled,
"The World's Plunderers. Germany, Britain, and Russia grab
what they can of Africa and Asia." The left figure holds a
sack that reads "German Grab-Bag"; the middle figure,
"British Grab-Bag"; the right figure, "Russian Grab-Bag."

17. The cartoon above reflects what 19th century global
process?

(A) The causes of the Opium Wars

(B) European imperialism

(C) The Industrial Revolution

(D) The rise of Marxism

18. Which of these was a principal factor that led to the 19th century global process depicted in the cartoon?

(A) Trade agreements between Germany, Britain, and Russia

(B) Military alliances with Germany, Britain, and Russia on one side, and Africa and Asia on the other

(C) The development of new transportation and medical technologies

(D) African and Asian demands for products from Europe

19. The region that was the primary focus and recipient of European imperialism in the 19th century was:

(A) The Americas

(B) Australia and New Zealand

(C) Southeast Asia

(D) Africa

Use the image below to answer questions 20–22.

Source: "Second World War British Propaganda Posters—in Pictures," The Guardian, Nov. 3, 2014.

20. This World War II poster, printed and distributed by the British government, promotes which of these concepts?

    (A) The extent of democracy throughout the British empire during World War II.

    (B) The patriarchal nature of the empire at the start of World War II.

    (C) The success of Britain's appeasement policy before World War II.

    (D) The global extent of the empire during World War II.

21. An opponent of the message portrayed in this poster would most likely be:

    (A) A Kenyan nationalist seeking self-rule

    (B) An Australian citizen who felt unthreatened by war

    (C) A British suffragette seeking equality

    (D) A Canadian citizen who was conscripted into the military

22. In the years after World War II, what was the status of the British empire?

    (A) It immediately collapsed as soon as the war ended in 1945.

    (B) It steadily declined in size over the next 25 years.

    (C) It maintained its status as the largest empire in the world.

    (D) It sold its colonial holdings to rising powers such as the United States and Soviet Union.

**Use the image below and your knowledge
of world history to answer questions 23–25.**

Cartoon by Illingworth, British "Daily Mail" newspaper, 1947

23. The cartoon above is best understood in the context of

(A) the Russian-German Non-Aggression pact during World War II

(B) free trade agreements between Eastern and Western Europe in the mid-20th century

(C) the growing popularity of Eastern European artistic styles in the post–World War II era

(D) Western European concerns about Soviet intentions after World War II

24. What was the most significant response to the focus of this cartoon by the U.S. and many Western European nations?

(A) They formed the European Coal and Steel Community and NAFTA.

(B) They formed NATO (the North Atlantic Treaty Organization).

(C) They encouraged Eastern European artists to sell their works to the West.

(D) They built a wall to separate East Germany from West Germany.

25. In which conflict did the United Nations authorize and commit troops to oppose forces supported by communist countries?

(A) Vietnam in the 1950s and 1960s

(B) Israel in the 1960s

(C) Korea in the 1950s

(D) Iraq in the 1990s

ANSWERS AND EXPLANATIONS

1. **(C)** The original Russian author's point of view was likely swayed in his opinions about the Mongols by stories of their conquest of his land. The translation to English (A) was written centuries after Mongol conquests. There is no evidence the original author was granted access by the Mongols to their documents (B). Contrary to the assertion in Choice (D), the Mongol written language was known to Westerners at least by Marco Polo's time (early 14th century).

2. **(A)** The Mongol empire was much larger than the Holy Roman Empire (B). It lasted about 200 years, while the Ottoman Empire lasted about 700 years (C). The Mongols failed in their attempts to invade Japan by sea, ending any thoughts of expansion further into the Pacific (D).

3. **(D)** Trade increased during the Age of the Mongols, and with trade came diseases, most notably the Black Death, which struck from China all the way to Europe because of trade routes. There is no historical basis for Choices (A) or (B). In addition, at no time in the 14th century was the medical community equipped to deal with the Black Death (C).

4. **(A)** The Reformation preceded the Enlightenment.

5. **(C)** The movement to end slavery was implemented in European colonies and spread to nations in the Americas. The other choices can be considered Enlightenment-inspired reforms, but none is abolitionism.

6. **(B)** Decolonization movements of the 20th century were sparked by nationalist fervor derived from Enlightenment concepts that had inspired nationalist movements in the 19th century. "Bollywood" movies were more a result of technology and the spread of American Hollywood movies (A). Fascism was highly nationalist politically, but its ideals were far removed from Enlightenment philosophy (C). The movement to restore some faiths to their basic teachings (D) was in some sense a response to some cultural outcomes of the Enlightenment, but not as directly as decolonization.

7. **(A)** World historians call this and similar blending of tradition syncretism. *Global migration* involves the moving of people, but not necessarily the blending of their cultures (B). *Nationalism* is pride in one's country and/or cultural heritage (C). *Theocracy* is government run under religious guidelines (D).

8. **(C)** Catholicism in Latin America strongly featured syncretism with indigenous beliefs. Mahayana Buddhism was more syncretic than Theravada Buddhism (A). Once established, Judaism incorporated little from nearby religions (B), especially compared to Catholicism in Latin America. Daoism is part of Chinese culture, not Russian (D).

9. **(D)** Choice (A) is incorrect because the era of European imperialism in Africa was the 19th century. Choice (B) is incorrect because such alliances did not exist with Spain at that time. And Choice (C) is incorrect because no such government programs existed on a large scale.

10. **(C)** Feudalism developed in western Europe centuries before 1848 (A) Mercantilism of the 16th–18th centuries had faded by the mid-19th century in western Europe in favor of free trade (B) Russia's communist revolution occurred in the early 20th century.

11. **(A)** For (B), (C), and (D), the opposite is true.

12. **(D)** (A) social welfare programs like British National Health System and Social Security in the U.S. (B)—communist revolutions in Russia, China by the mid-20th century (C). The Cold War began approximately one year after the end of World War II in 1946.

13. **(C)** (A) and (B) are not historically accurate. Communism fell in Eastern Europe, including Russia in the late 20th century. Communist China began implementing some capitalist reforms at the same time. (D) is not accurate because nations such as Cuba and North Korea remained firmly communist at the end of the 20th century.

14. **(B)** The Columbian exchange began as a trans-Atlantic process in the late 15th century and spread to the Indian Ocean region and East Asia soon after. The Industrial Revolution reached Japan in the 19th century (A), as did Social Darwinism (C) and the concept of the "White Man's Burden" (D).

15. **(A)** Capitalism encourages free trade; mercantilism encourages protectionism (B). Socialism developed in the 19th century (C). Nationalism is a sense of pride of one's ethnicity, language and culture (D).

16. **(C)** The Bakufu was the government in Japan headed by a shogun (A). The Greater East Asia C-Prosperity Sphere was an imperial Japanese policy from 1930–1945 (B). The Samurai were the warrior class that had significant power until the Meiji government (D).

17. **(B)** The Opium Wars focused on a trade dispute between China and Britain (A). The Industrial Revolution and the rise of Marxism are not the focus of the cartoon (C, D).

18. **(C)** Steamboats, trains, and improved medicines made the "new" imperialism of the 19th century into previously uncolonized regions possible. The cartoon does not refer to trade agreements (A) or military alliances (B). The opposite was true for Choice (D).

19. **(D)** The Americas were initially colonized by Europeans beginning in the late 15th century (A). Australia and New Zealand were colonized by Europeans largely in the 18th century (B). Southeast Asia did see European colonization in the 19th century but not to the extent of Africa (C).

20. **(D)** Democracy was not practiced throughout the British empire (A). Patriarchy is not a focus of this war poster (B). Britain's appeasement policy was not a success (C).

21. **(A)** There was a large nationalist-based independence movement in Kenya in the mid-20th century. Some nationalists there opposed assisting the British in World War II. Australians were under a real threat of Japanese invasion (B). Choices (C) and (D) represent people who would be more likely to put aside their differences with British empire policies during World War II than someone from an African or Asian colony.

22. **(B)** beginning with the independence of India and its partition in 1949 through the hand-over of Hong Kong in 1997. The other choices are historically inaccurate.

23. **(D)** The Russian-German Non-Aggression pact was agreed to in 1941 (A). Free trade agreements did not exist during the Cold War (B). The cartoon has nothing to do with admiration of artistic styles (C).

24. **(B)** Choice (A) is incorrect because the European Coal and Steel Community was a free-trade agreement between some Western European nations, and NAFTA was a trade agreement between the U.S., Canada, and Mexico in the 1990s. Choice (C) has no basis in fact. Choice (D) alludes to the Berlin Wall, a barrier erected by the Soviet-backed East German government in 1961 to separate East Berlin from West Berlin.

25. **(C)** The United Nations did not authorize the use of its troops in Vietnam (A) or Israel (B). The UN use of force in Iraq was not against communism (D).

Tackling the
Short-Answer Questions

After triumphing over the multiple-choice section of the exam, you will move on to conquer the short-answer questions. You will have 40 minutes to answer three out of four questions. Questions 1 and 2 will have stimulus items, such as a map, a historical document or quotes from historians with different points of view on a development in history. You will be asked to respond based on your knowledge of world history and on your ability to use the learning objectives and historical thinking skills you have developed. The short-answer section is worth 20% of the exam.

Questions 1 and 2 are **required** and will come from the years 1200 to 2001. (See chapters 4–12). Question 1 will assess your ability to work with a secondary source, such as a historian's argument, that is connected to a historical event or process. Question 2 will feature a primary source connected to a historical event or process.

You will then answer *either* question 3 (from 1200 to 1750) or question 4 (from 1750 to 2001). Neither will have a stimulus attached.

The four main historical periods of AP® World History: Modern will be covered in these four short-answer questions.

Each short-answer question has 3 parts: a, b, and c. Each part is worth 1 point. It will help the exam grader (and therefore, you) to **label your answers a), b), and c)** and write *only* the response for that particular part. You don't need a thesis statement; just address exactly what questions a, b, and c are asking.

Usually, short-answer questions ask for an *explanation*. That means you must include the significance or "because " in your answer. Look at the sample below. The second and third sentences in "a" include an explanation.

Also, you must write *only inside the box* that is provided for that question. Graders are not allowed to read anything outside the box. Picture a text box about three-fourths of a page long, with lines for writing. You don't have to fill in the whole box as long as you are fully answering the question, but remember, like the DBQ and the long essay, the short-answer questions are scored based on what you get right, and the wrong stuff is ignored. So write! After you finish the short-answer section, you will have a brief break. Then, it's on to the essays.

Here is an example of a short-answer question and a good response:

Question:

Use the excerpt below and your knowledge of world history to answer all parts of the question that follows.
"[The soldier] stood upon a little mound,
Cast his lethargic eyes around,
And said beneath his breath:
'Whatever happens we have got
The Maxim Gun, and they have not.'
He marked them in their rude advance,
He hushed their rebel cheers;
With one extremely vulgar glance
He broke the Mutineers . . . .
We shot and hanged a few, and then
The rest became devoted men . . . .
While they support us, we should lend
Our every effort to defend,
And from a higher point of view
To give the full direction due
To all the native races."

—Hilaire Belloc, British author and politician,
The Modern Traveler, 1898

a) Briefly explain the historical context of this poem.

b) Describe and explain ONE specific example of native resistance in Africa to the events depicted in this poem.

c) Describe and explain ONE specific example of native resistance in Asia to the events depicted in this poem.

Sample Response note that each answer is labeled a, b or c.

a) The historical context of this poem is 19th century European imperialism of Africa and Asia. Europeans believed themselves to be superior to natives and felt they had a right to conquer them. Social Darwinism and strong nationalism fueled this attitude.

b) One example from Africa was when the Zulu warriors attacked British outposts in southern Africa. Even though the Africans won a major battle, the British did not leave the region. This represented the peak of Zulu resistance.

c) One example from Asia was the Indian Mutiny, or Sepoy Rebellion in the 19th century, when anti-British Indian soldiers fought pro-British Indians and the British army. As in Africa, this rebellion failed to get the British to leave, in this case because Britain had the support of many Indian soldiers.

Mastering the Document-Based Question

Your multiple-choice and short-answer sections have been turned in; you've had a short break. Next you'll face the Document-Based Question and the Long Essay Question. Both types of essays will be "to-what-extent" questions. The point is to show that history is not all one-sided. ALL the Mongols weren't evil ALL the time, just like ALL your teachers aren't mean ALL the time. Sometimes, like the Mongols, your teachers can be nice.

You have to prove to the exam graders that you understand that history was, "mostly *this*; however, there was a little of *that*."

The DBQ and LEQ items will address Comparison (similarities and/or differences) or Causation (causes and/or effects) or Continuity and Change.

Examples of DBQ or LEQ essay prompts:

- **Comparison essay:** "Develop an argument that evaluates the extent to which Japanese and Chinese responses to western influences in the 19th century were similar."

  One way to address this question is to develop an argument that Japan and China were mostly different in their responses to Western influences in the 19th century. For example, Japan adopted a Western-style constitutional monarchy and China did not. However, there were some similarities, such as both tried to maintain their independence from Western colonialism.

- **Causation essay:** "To what extent did the Industrial Revolution contribute to the high casualties in World War I?"

  Here you could develop an argument that to a great extent, technology from the Industrial Revolution like the machine gun caused high casualties in World War I. To a lesser extent, the war lasted so long and millions died because of the refusal by the leaders on all sides to negotiate a peace early in the war.

- **Continuity and Change essay:** "Evaluate the extent of change in religious traditions in the Americas from c. 1500 to c. 1750."

A good response would develop an essay that argued that there was a great deal of change in religious traditions in the Americas after the introduction of Christianity by Europeans, but that some continuities remained, such as the blending of some African practices with Christianity to form Vodun ("Voodoo").

Did you notice that all these responses include "a lot of *this* but a little of *that*"? You can practice by writing essays that compare two friends—How they are they mostly similar, but have some differences. Or, which is greater, continuities or changes in your own life in the past five years? "I am mostly the same in where I live and what I eat; however, I am a little different in what I wear." Then provide specific examples and explain why.

These writing concepts will help you learn how to approach the DBQ and LEQ.

It's easy to check on your progress as you work through the DBQ and the long essay. Just above the question on the exam, you will see bulleted reminders of the scoring rubric. Check off each bullet as you complete the corresponding task in your essay.

The DBQ is the first essay you'll encounter, and it is also the most difficult to master. However, thousands of students do well on it—why not you?

The Document-Based Question is just that—a question with documents. Your job is to incorporate the documents and your knowledge of world history into an essay that addresses *all* parts of the question. It is worth 25% of your total score. You will have 60 minutes to write it, which includes a 15-minute prep period. There will be seven documents that you must discuss, organize and analyze. The DBQ will cover historical developments or processes from somewhere between the years 1450 and 2001.

The DBQ is scored on a scale up to 7 points. Few essays earn a 7, so don't worry about that. Just follow these tips, practice writing, and do your best. Each DBQ point is equal to about five multiple-choice questions, so keep that in mind as you prepare. Every rubric point is a big deal.

You'll find a DBQ with the online practice exam available with this book (see inside front cover).

The rubric requires you to do the following:

(1) Have a thesis that addresses all parts of the question with an argument or line of reasoning, with examples showing "a lot of this; but, a little of that."

(2) Put the question into historical context.

(3) Correctly incorporate and explain the significance of at least 6 of the 7 documents in direct response to the question (up to 2 points).

(4) Include at least one example of outside information not found in the documents that connects to the question.

(5) Discuss point-of-view (POV) (Why did they create it? How do they know what they're talking about? Who is the intended audience?) with at least 3 documents.

(6) Show "complexity" in your essay. Analyze both similarities AND differences, or continuity AND change, or causes AND effects, or perhaps compare what happened in the era of the question to another era in world history.

Point total: 7

Test Tip

AP® World History exam readers don't start at 7 points and knock off points for mistakes. They begin at zero and add points for things you do correctly. Exam readers realize that this is a high-pressure exam and that your essay is a first draft. They read beyond your mistakes and assign points based on what you did right.

HOW TO APPROACH THE DBQ

FIRST:

Read the question. Pause. Take a deep breath. Read it again, slower this time. Make sure you *understand and underline all the tasks of the question.*

SECOND:

Make a list of historical developments that pop into your head from the era of the question. You can access this as a source of outside information in the essay. The folks who create the DBQ purposefully leave out key information in the Source line of each document to push you into thinking about outside information. The Source line might say, "A letter from Mohandas Gandhi." Your job would be to add outside information about the historical significance of Gandhi.

THIRD:

Tackle the documents. Discuss, analyze, and organize the documents. Read them, make notes in the margins on what each one says. Organize them into "a lot of this" and "a little of that," based on the prompt. Next: What is significant about each document? You can force yourself to answer that question by writing, "This shows . . . " about each document in your essay.

Look for Point of View (POV): For what purpose was this document made: to persuade, intimidate, or even trick someone? *Or* . . . Does this person really know what they're talking about? *Or* . . . Who is the intended audience of the document? *Or* . . . Describe the document's tone: angry? submissive? confused? ANY of these could count for POV.

Now you are ready to write the essay. Note: The exam graders aren't looking for exactly the format that follows. Think of this as a guide to help you sort through the essay writing process.

THE DBQ ESSAY

Thesis: Includes (1) all parts of the question with specific examples and (2) makes a historically defensible claim that establishes a line of reasoning. Your thesis MUST be at the beginning or at the end of your essay. Graders know you are under pressure, so if your first thesis attempt falls short, they go to the end of the essay and look for an acceptable statement in your conclusion.

EXAMPLE:

A prompt that asks you to evaluate the extent to which globalization caused economic changes in Asia after World War II might start with this thesis:

> There was a great deal of economic change in Asia after World War II due to globalization, for example the rise of the "Asian Tigers" like South Korea. However, some parts of Asia seemed isolated from these changes, like in rural parts of western China and Afghanistan." See? A lot of *this* ("a great deal"); however, a little of *that* ("some parts").

Of course, the content of the documents will guide you through the creation of your thesis.

Paragraph 2, Context: Briefly put the topic of the question in historical context.

1. How did we get to the beginning point of the question? In this example, briefly define the term, "globalization," and where Asia fit into that process at the end of World War II.

2. You could also briefly describe other big social/cultural/ political/or environmental processes that were happening in the era of the question. This information must connect to the question in some way

   > "World War II was the biggest and worst war in history. Much of Asia was fought over, and at the end, the economies of countries like Japan and China were totally ruined. Programs promoted by communist and capitalist countries tried to rebuild the world into their image and pull Asia and the rest of the world into global markets."

   > *Or . . .*

   > "World War II brought huge leaps in technology in communication and transportation. These advancements led to increased global markets, connecting Asia to the rest of the world in new and bigger ways."

The next paragraphs discuss, analyze, and organize the documents in response to the question.

A. Name your first group/argument ("a lot of this") with a topic sentence that introduces this paragraph;

   Here's an example: "Globalization created many economic changes in Asia after WWII."

B. Name the source of each document (who said/wrote it?)

   Example: "Changes included rapid industrialization, as seen in Doc 1, a speech by the president of Korea in 1988."

C. Tell the reader what each document represents and its significance to your argument in your own words. Quoting from the document is not necessary. (AP® graders want to see that you are "wrestling" with the document and not just repeating it)

To continue from the example above in B: "He says that without globalization, Korea would still be a third world country. This shows how far Korea advanced economically after the Korean War." Remember, you need not spend time re-writing the quotes from a document. Summarize the author's thoughts and include, "This shows . . . ."

D. Attach point-of-view (POV) to as many documents as you can in this group. (See earlier POV discussion.)

Continuing from the example above in C: "As Korea's leader, he is proud of his country's changes. His speech was before a crowd of supporters, who clearly agreed with his views."

E. Include information not found in the documents (outside information) relevant to your argument. Look for hints in the Source line of the documents and in the list you made of events during the era of the question.

One way to do this in the example you've been following: "South Korea's economy boomed in the late 20th century greatly because of huge support from the U.S. and creative Korean entrepreneurs."

In a new paragraph, address your "a little of that" group of documents and arguments in the same way as your "a lot of this" group. In this example, a topic sentence could be:

> "However, in some places in Asia, globalization caused little economic change after WWII." And go from there, using the examples above as your guide: Document analysis, POV, outside information.

Address both sides of the question. ("Complexity")

If there is a question about similarities and differences or continuities and changes, in many cases, you handled this in your "a lot of this; however, a little of that" analysis. But look back and make sure, especially if the question is about causes or effects. This is the place in a "causes" essay to talk briefly about a couple of specific effects, and vice versa.

Finally, write a conclusion that addresses all parts of the question with specific examples. It might count as your thesis if the one at the beginning of your essay falls short.

If you finish your essay ahead of the 60-minute time frame, review your work and make any necessary corrections. AP® readers understand it's a first-draft essay in a high-pressure situation. If you have extra time, don't waste it—add information, cross stuff out, and revise whole paragraphs, if you need to. You can even write new material, circle it, draw an arrow where it's supposed to go, and put "insert here" on the DBQ and long essay.

DBQ Musts for 7 points:

- You must have an acceptable thesis.

- You must have a discussion of context.

- You must discuss and analyze at least 6 documents. (2 points).

- You must have at least 3 POV (points of view).

- You must discuss at least 1 example of outside information.

- You must show "complexity" in your argument.

Tips for Writing the Long Essay

Like in the DBQ the types of long essays you will see on the AP® World History: Modern exam include: Comparison (similarities and differences), Causation (cause and/or effect), and Continuity and Change Over Time.

You will be given three long-essay prompts, *but choose only one essay topic.* Instructions will tell you to pick *one* long essay prompt from 1200 to 1750, *or* 1450 to 1900, *or* 1750 to 2001.

The long essay is graded on a 6-point scale. You are allotted 40 minutes to prepare and write it, for 15% of your overall grade. Here are the basic rubric points for the long essay:

➤ **Thesis/Claim (1 point):** Present a thesis that makes a historically defensible claim or that establishes a line of reasoning, responding to all parts of the question. The thesis must consist of one or more sentences located in one place, either in the introduction or the conclusion.

➤ **Contextualization (1 point):** Describe a broader historical context relevant to the prompt.

➤ **Evidence (1 or 2 points):** Support an argument in response to the prompt using specific and relevant examples.

➤ **Analysis and Reasoning (1 or 2 points):** Demonstrate a complex understanding of the historical development in the prompt to support, qualify, or modify an argument.

All AP® World History: Modern long essays are **argumentative** because you must take a stand based on the prompt ("a historically defensible claim") and provide evidence and arguments to support your stand. For example, a prompt could read:

"Evaluate the extent to which new technology influenced change in Africa in the era c. 1750–c. 1900."

A successful essay could argue that technology fostered a lot of change ("a lot of" being a minimal "extent-to-which" argument) in c. 1750–c. 1900, but you must also provide examples of things that didn't change despite technology ("On the other hand, not everything changed in Africa in this era because of new technology. For example . . . ") That "extent to which" business in the prompt is telling you to pick a side to argue, but to earn full credit, you must discuss and analyze the opposite argument as well.

The side you pick isn't crucial as long as you can support your argument with facts and analysis. The goal is to show complexity in your thinking, and not write about history being all one way or the other.

Students often ask, "How many specific pieces of evidence must I offer?" The answer is: as many as you can think of.

AP® history is not about how little you can do to get credit. AP® history is about showing how much you know. If some of your "evidence" is wrong, graders don't count points off. They only score what you get right. So load up on evidence!

Avoid extreme terms like "everyone," "always," "all," "nobody," "never," and "none." Instead, use qualified words such as "most," "usually," "sometimes," "rarely," and "a few." For example, "Everything in Africa changed because of new technology." Really? You know for a fact that every . . . single . . . thing in Africa changed because of trains and new medicine? Of course not. That's why, "Many things in Africa changed after the introduction of new technology in the era 1750–1900," is a more defensible argument.

The next section includes "how to" guides for success on the AP® World History: Modern long essay question. Walk through them one at a time to get comfortable with the requirements for the different types of long essays.

"HOW TO" GUIDES FOR SUCCESS ON THE LONG ESSAY

Test Tip

Important! You must adapt these suggestions to fit the terms of the question.

1. The Comparison Long Essay

This sample essay prompt echoes the one from the beginning of Chapter 20: "Analyze the extent to which Japanese and Chinese responses to Western influences in the 19th century were similar."

One approach is to develop an argument that Japan and China were mostly different in their responses to western influences by 1900. For example, Japan adopted a Western-style constitutional monarchy and China did not. However, there were some similarities, such as both tried to maintain their independence from Western colonialism.

You don't "have to" have paragraphs, but the exam grader will be grateful for them.

Paragraph 1 Thesis: "There were more similarities but some differences in (name the two things/eras/events being compared). For example, there were similarities in (provide two examples). However, there were also some differences in . . . ." .

Example thesis: There were more differences than similarities in how Japan and China responded to 19th century western influences. Japan brought in the Industrial Revolution and a constitutional monarchy while China mostly resisted Westernization. However, both countries sent people to the West to learn their ways."

Paragraph 2: Put the question in historical **context**. What was happening in this question's world that brought us to this question.

Example context: "European countries and the U.S. were growing in power in the 19th century because of new industrial might. Competition for markets around the world fed a spirit of imperialism. Japan and China were targets of western economic and political interests and they responded to these new potential threats."

Paragraph 3: Evidence with analysis

Topic sentence: "There were more differences than similarities in how Japan and China responded to Westernization."

Provide examples of differences: Japan yielded to the Western powers and China resisted by fighting the Opium wars to stop British influence. Japan began the Meiji Restoration, a Western-style government while China stuck with their ancient system. Japan began a fast-paced Industrial Revolution but China was slow to industrialize. (These are just some examples, I bet you have more.)

Next, analyze *why* they responded differently:

"Japan saw how China fought Britain and lost, so they decided it was better to switch than fight. China was the greatest economic power in the world in 1800, so they believed they could push back against the latest threat and win, but by 1900, it was too late." (These are just some examples; I bet you have more.)

Paragraph 4: Evidence with analysis

Topic sentence: "On the other hand, there were some similarities in how Japan and China responded to Westernization by 1900."

Evidence: "For example, both countries sent people to the West to learn about them. Japan and China hired foreign experts to help modernize their militaries, and both faced opposition inside their countries to their government's official policies on Westernization."

Next, analyze *why* they responded similarly:

"Japan and China sent people to the West because they figured the best way to deal with an outside threat was to study them. They hired foreign military experts because Europe and the U.S. had more modern weapons, and these Asian countries wanted to be stronger."

Paragraph 5: Conclusion

A conclusion isn't mandatory, but it's a good idea to reword your thesis here, just in case the one at the start of your essay isn't quite enough to earn the point. Scoring: Thesis (1), Context (1), Lots of specific evidence that responds to the prompt (2), Complex argument (2)—explains the significance of the evidence and argues both sides of the question.

2. **The Causation Long Essay (causes and/or effects of an event or movement, for example)**

Let's look at the causation prompt near the beginning of Chapter 20:

"To what extent did the Industrial Revolution contribute to the high casualties in World War I?"

Paragraph 1 Thesis: "There were many causes (or effects) of (name the event). Perhaps the most important causes (or effects) were _____ and _____ because of their great effects on history. However, other factors were also causes, such as _____."

Example: "To a great extent, technology from the Industrial Revolution like the machine gun and submarines caused high casualties in WWI. However, the refusal by the leaders on all sides to negotiate a peace early in the war also led to a long and bloody war."

Paragraph 2: Context. Define the event and put it in historical context. What was happening in this question's world? Example: "World War I began because of 50 years of competition among the Great Powers of Europe for land and resources around the world. This led to secret alliances and huge military build-ups, which increased tensions to the breaking point by the early 20th century. The killing of the Archduke of Austria-Hungary led to a chain of events that nobody seemed to want to stop."

Paragraph 3: Evidence with analysis. Discuss as many specific causes and/or effects (depending on the question) of the event as you can think of. Name the *most* significant cause (or effect) and tell *why* it is significant.

Topic sentence: "The greatest reason why WWI was so deadly was the new weapons that came out of the Industrial Revolution."

Evidence: Discuss the effects of the machine gun, submarine, poison gas, long-range cannon, the airplane, the tank . . . you get the point.

Next, analyze *why* these new weapons were so deadly: "The machine gun shot so fast that men had no chance against them. The generals kept using old tactics of marching men in straight lines across the battlefield, and they were slaughtered every time." I bet you have more examples.

Paragraph 4: Evidence with analysis

Topic sentence: "On the other hand, some of the high casualties were not due just to new weapons from the Industrial Revolution."

Evidence: "Secret treaties from before the war and the stubborn refusal of the nations to end it before it got way out of hand were other reasons why it got so bad." I bet you can think of more reasons, like national pride.

Next analyze *why* the nations refused to negotiate a quick end to the war: "Due to imperial rivalries in Africa between Germany, Britain, France, and suspicions between the Kaiser of Germany and the Czar of Russia, nobody was interested in talking peace until millions had died."

Paragraph 5 Conclusion. A conclusion isn't mandatory, but it's a good idea to reword your thesis here, just in case the one at the start of your essay isn't quite enough to earn the point.

Scoring: Thesis (1), Context (1), Lots of specific Evidence that responds to the prompt (2), Complex argument (2)—explains the significance of the evidence and argues both sides of the question.

3. **The Continuity and Change Over Time Long Essay**

It is important to address the time period named in the CCOT prompt. Otherwise, how can you show change over time without naming the time?

Here is the CCOT prompt found at the beginning of Chapter 20:

"Evaluate the extent of change in religious traditions in the Americas from c. 1500 to c. 1750."

A strong response would develop an essay that argued that there was much change in religious traditions in the Americas after the introduction of Christianity by Europeans, but that some continuities remained, such as the blending of some indigenous African religious practices with Christianity to form Vodun ("Voodoo").

Paragraph 1: Thesis. "There were many continuities and some changes (or, more changes than continuities if that works for you) in (insert the time and topic of the question). Provide some specific examples of both continuity and change in your thesis."

Example: "There was a great deal of change in religious traditions in the Americas from c. 1500 through c. 1750, like a shift to monotheism after Christianity was introduced from Europe; however, some traditions continued, like the secret worship of the old gods."

Paragraph 2: Context. Define the topic and put it in historical context. What was happening elsewhere in the world at this time?

Example: "Throughout history, religions have spread and as they often did, they changed to fit local traditions. When Islam moved into South Asia, it accommodated the large majority of Hindus by making them "the people of the Book." Changes to religion also occurred in the Americas with the arrival of Christian conquistadors."

Paragraph 3: Evidence with analysis. Discuss as many specific examples of changes (or continuities) during the time period and topic of the question as you can come up with.

Topic sentence: "There were many changes in the religious traditions in the Americas after the arrival of the Europeans c. 1500."

Examples: Shift from polytheism to monotheism through the introduction of Christianity by European missionaries, a loss of influence of the indigenous priests, the removal of Aztec and Inca kings as gods. (I bet you can think of more.)

Next, analyze *why* these changes occurred: As Native Americans began to die in large numbers, their old ways died too; the Spanish and Portuguese had a strong missionary desire to convert the natives to their faith; it made good sense for the overwhelmed natives to convert to the faith of the dominant European outsiders. (I bet you can think of more.)

Paragraph 4: Evidence with analysis. Now discuss some specific examples of the other side of the argument. If you choose changes in paragraph 3, then write about continuities in paragraph 4. Continuities do not have to cover the entire era, just most of it. But you have to state that in your essay: "For most of this era this stayed the same, but it changed when . . . ."

Topic sentence: "However, some religious traditions in the Americas continued."

Examples: In Latin America, the Virgin of Guadalupe incorporated elements of the Aztec religion into Catholicism. In the Caribbean, African immigrants blended their culture's faith with Catholicism to form Vodun.

Next, analyze *why* these beliefs remained: "This happened because it is very difficult for people to completely abandon long-held beliefs. In Latin America, many Christian missionaries looked the other way when they saw natives practicing their old ways because it was just too hard to police everybody."

Paragraph 5: Conclusion. A conclusion isn't mandatory, but it's wise to reword your thesis here, just in case the one at the beginning of your essay isn't strong enough to earn the point. Scoring: Thesis (1), Context (1), Lots of specific Evidence that responds to the prompt (2), Complex argument (2)—explains the significance of the evidence and argues both sides of the question.

Long Essay "Musts" for 6 points

- You must have an acceptable thesis.

- You must have a discussion of context.

- You must discuss and analyze specific historical evidence. (2 points)

- You must show a complex understanding of the question. (2 points)

Test Tip

Final Note: *It is to your advantage to repeat the terms of the question throughout your essay.*

Don't get fancy with synonyms for similarities and differences, cause or effect, or continuity and change. You want the essay reader to concentrate on your arguments, not fancy synonyms.

Countdown Calendar

Here's a countdown calendar of preparation tips for the AP® World History: Modern exam.

SIX WEEKS BEFORE THE EXAM

➤ Read this book cover to cover and pay attention to its advice. Remember, always keep the big picture of AP® World History: Modern's themes in mind.

➤ Go to *www.rea.com/studycenter* and take the free online practice exam to find out where your strengths and weaknesses lie. Focus your remaining study time on your weaker areas.

➤ Find and answer previously released AP® World History essay questions since 2017 with topics after 1200 CE and write, write, write.

FOUR WEEKS BEFORE THE EXAM

➤ Review your study materials daily to keep the material and skills fresh in your mind. Pay special attention to Parts I and II of this book to increase and sharpen your content knowledge.

TWO WEEKS BEFORE THE EXAM

➤ Quiz yourself on the rubrics for each essay and commit them to memory.

➤ Review your study materials every night to keep the material and skills fresh in your mind, adding Part III to your continued study of Parts I and II.

ONE DAY BEFORE THE EXAM

➤ Reread Chapter 1 of this *Crash Course* and then get a good night's sleep—at least 8 hours. It's important to wake up fresh in the morning. If you've paid close attention to the advice in this book, relax. You are prepared for success!

THE DAY OF THE EXAM

➤ Take a shower and put on clothes. Don't laugh, some people get really nervous! Not you, though. You've been studying this book.

➤ Plan to show up at the exam site at least 20 minutes before the scheduled start time for the test.

➤ Bring two fresh No. 2 pencils with clean erasers and two working blue- or black-ink pens.

➤ Bring a snack and a bottle of water for the break after the short-answer questions.

➤ Be prepared to turn off and turn in your cell phone and other electronic devices before the exam.

➤ The exam proctor will read a lot of instructions—be patient. Plan to spend about 4 hours at the exam site.

➤ Answer every multiple-choice question, even if you have to guess, and all parts of each essay. Remember, you get points for what is right and the graders ignore what's wrong. Every point counts!

➤ When you're finished, treat yourself to some fun time with friends. There's probably a big movie that just hit the theaters.

Notes

Notes

Notes

Notes

Notes

Notes

Notes

Notes